"If insecurity has ev~~~~~~~~~~, rearranged your vision, or crushed your confidence, *Living in the Power of My Weakness* is a fresh reminder that God provides everything you need to complete the work he's given you. This book will change your life and the lives of those you influence."

—Gwen Smith
Speaker, Worship Leader, Author of *Broken into Beautiful*

"In a great paradox of the divine, we are destined to be more than conquerors, and this is accomplished through our weakness. With the heart of a servant and the gift of a storyteller, Dave Clark describes the mystery of who we are in Christ and the majesty of Christ in us. You will be comforted, challenged, and encouraged as he points you back to the mighty God we serve."

—Randy Vader
PraiseGathering Music

"If you want to know about grace, listen to someone who has walked the hard roads with Christ—read my good friend Dave Clark's story in *Living in the Power of My Weakness*. It just might save a step or two on your own journey."

—Mike Harland
Director, LifeWay Worship

"Using the engaging style so apparent in his song lyrics, Dave Clark has crafted a spiritual encounter and a source of reflection that you will want to keep close at hand. This is a book you'll want to buy for others after you've read it yourself. Let it soak in—it will change you!"

—Jesse C. Middendorf
Director, Center for Pastoral Leadership
Nazarene Theological Seminary

"Dave Clark has crafted an honest, heartfelt book that will speak to the souls of pastors, worship leaders, counselors, teachers, and mentors. Dave's devotion to the Lord and love for the Church drives him to share dynamic principles for servant leadership that are deeply rooted in Scripture, Christian disciplines, and evangelical tradition. *Living in the Power of My Weakness* is a must-read for anyone in ministry."

—Dr. Vernon M. Whaley
Dean, Liberty University School of Music

living in
the power
OF MY
weakness

DAVE CLARK

Inspiration for Ministry Leaders

BEACON HILL PRESS
OF KANSAS CITY

Copyright © 2014 by Dave Clark
Beacon Hill Press of Kansas City
PO Box 419527
Kansas City, MO 64141
www.beaconhillbooks.com

ISBN 978-0-8341-3359-4
Printed in the
United States of America

Cover Design: Nathan Johnson
Interior Design: Sharon Page

Library of Congress Cataloguing-in-Publication Data
Clark, Dave, 1958- author.
  Living in the power of my weakness : inspiration for ministry leaders / Dave Clark.
    pages cm
  Includes bibliographical references.
  ISBN 978-0-8341-3359-4 (pbk.)
  1. Pastoral theology. I. Title.
  BV4011.2.C53 2014
  242'.692—dc23
                                                              2014021475

10 9 8 7 6 5 4 3 2 1

Contents

Acknowledgments

I am blessed to be surrounded by those who love me, encourage me and compel me to reach beyond my weaknesses. To each of you I am indebted.

Those I work with—Melanie Harris, Michael Cork, Emily Higinbotham, Chasity Phillips, Heather Knight, Chris Robinette, Mike Harland, Gabriele Udell and Donna Goodrich (1 Corinthians 3:7-9).

Those I live with—Cindi, Allison, Anna and Sam—day after day we watch each other grow and I am better for the journey. I hope these pages give you a deeper understanding of the way I go about it (James 1:16-18).

The one I serve—"You have searched me, Lord, and you know me. You know when I sit and when I rise; you perceive my thoughts from afar. You discern my going out and my lying down; you are familiar with all my ways. Before a word is on my tongue you, Lord, know it completely. You hem me in behind and before, and you lay your hand upon me. Such knowledge is too wonderful for me, too lofty for me to attain" (Psalm 139:1-6, NIV).

Foreword

No one wants to admit they are weak. The world we live in doesn't reward weakness. Instead, it elevates and promotes the strong. We are taught as youngsters to be tough and stand up to the people that confront us. We are admonished to "man up" when bullies invade our space. To indicate weakness is a weakness in itself, and therefore, vulnerability is to be avoided. Phrases like "never let them see you sweat" and "leadership projects confidence" promote a mindset in which we can never appear afraid or out of control.

Yet Paul, arguably the greatest of Christian evangelists, told the Corinthian church, "I will boast all the more gladly about my weaknesses, so that Christ's power may rest on me" (2 Cor. 12:9, NIV).

My friend Dave Clark embraces this teaching. Many of the songs we have co-written over the last 22 years reflect our own life experiences. Even today, our writing sessions usually start with the two of us sharing where life has taken us since we last met. Before we rhyme a word or turn a phrase, we converse about what's going on in our lives. Those conversations have been just as enjoyable to me as the songwriting. They have created a life-long friendship.

As with most of us, Dave's life has contained some dark chapters. Our conversations have included talk of cancer, sickness, struggle, disappointment, and fear. We have talked about our kids, our spouses, and our aging parents. Generally, these topics lead to sharing about not just our joys, but our struggles and the battles of daily life and ministry.

Like Paul, Dave has decided that the right thing to is to share his weaknesses so that Christ's power may be on display. Dave doesn't hide the struggles and pain behind his hit songs, his many awards, and the tremendous respect of his industry peers. This daring choice requires him to take off the mask of success and let people see behind the curtain. It requires that he willingly share the good, the bad, and the ugly from his reservoir of life experiences.

I applaud his candor and forthrightness. I respect the honesty that it requires—not many people are willing to be that authentic. Dave's courage allows the rest of us to look at our own life experiences and say, "I've felt that way too. Maybe I'm not so wrong for experiencing feelings of insecurity." After all, part of songwriting is realizing that you have either lived the lyrics or will live the lyrics before your life song has ended.

I encourage you to draw from Dave's well of experience, to learn from someone who has been there and chooses to share the journey rather than hide his struggles in the end results. I believe these words will give hope to those of us who think we are called to the big leagues before we are ready.

Does any of this sound familiar to you? Have you sensed God asking you to do something beyond the scope of your own abilities? In the trenches of daily ministry, have you questioned whether your efforts are making a difference? Do you project external confidence but experience a paralyzing inward fear when the quiet of the night finally closes in?

Take courage, my friend! This book is for you. You are stronger than you think. And it's not because of you—it's because he lives in you. In your weakness, he is strong.

Dan Dean, lead singer of Phillips, Craig, and Dean

Introduction

My name is Dave and I am a Christ-follower and a storyteller. I have borrowed from life's remnants left scattered along church pews and living rooms, failed pursuits, and radiant sunsets. I am not the first to recognize the evidence of sufficient grace in my life any more than I will be the last to write of its hold on me.

The concept for this book was conceived on a battlefield somewhere between God's will and my weakness. The actual writing could not begin, however, until I moved to a place of surrender where I could hear what God had been trying to tell me all along. The matter of measuring up to the call was never about my strength or abilities to begin with. It always was and still is about his power working through my weaknesses.

The pages that follow reflect the steps of an all-too-human seeker on a journey to know more about the God I have served since childhood but continue to discover each day. I write not as one who claims to understand the deep mysteries of the call, but rather as one who has yielded to its leading. The more I learn, the more I appreciate the beauty of Paul's prayer in Ephesians 3— that the Church would have the power to understand just how deep and how wide God's love really is. The more I see him, the more I learn about who I am.

Yes, I am inadequate, but I have been made a conqueror. I am vulnerable, yet I am not alone. I am weak, but through Christ I have been given access to the power of the Creator. In Colossians 2:9 we are promised that "in Christ all the fullness of the Deity lives in bodily form" (NIV). Any wisdom, any righteousness, any holiness is not the result of anything I have done or will ever do in the future. It is only the power of Christ working through me.

Perhaps you too have felt overwhelmed by the places God has called you to serve. Maybe your struggle is one of bondage to past failures or fear of the unknown. Maybe you wonder if the voice you hear calling is truly the Father's and, if so, why you still feel unworthy of the task at hand. You are not alone with your questions. From the church parking lot to the pulpit, Sunday to Sunday, the mission of the Church is carried out by people like you and me who feel daunted by the task, yet continue to find strength beyond our own.

The good news is that God doesn't wait until we have all our questions answered or our insecurities conquered before he calls us. It is not for us to determine our readiness to serve or debate what we have to offer to the building of his Kingdom. It is enough that he has uniquely and distinctly called each of us despite our issues, infirmities, doubts, and worries. He has found us worthy.

"But he said to me, 'My grace is sufficient for you, for my power is made perfect in weakness.' Therefore I will boast all the more gladly about my weaknesses, so that Christ's power may rest on me. That is why, for Christ's sake, I delight in weaknesses, in insults, in hardships, in persecutions, in difficulties. For when I am weak, then I am strong." (2 Corinthians 12:9-10, NIV)

ONE

When God Chooses You

Ye have not chosen me, but I have chosen you, and ordained you,
that ye should go and bring forth fruit, and that your fruit should
remain: that whatsoever ye shall ask of the Father in my name,
he may give it you (John 15:16, KJV).

April 16, 2007: The news of the day was dominated by a campus massacre at Virginia Tech. One lone gunman on a rampage ended more than thirty stories before the best chapters had been written. Cameras captured still-trembling eyewitnesses, grieving roommates, and parents learning how to mourn. Reporters, at a loss for new adjectives, resorted to the familiar ones, filling the silence with words like "senseless," "tragic," and "unimaginable." Like most of the country that night, I wrestled with a heart that hurt for those I didn't know as I searched for words I would never get the chance to say.

Our son, Sam, who was five years old at the time and oblivious to the nation's heartache, occupied himself with his nightly baseball game. To him, all that mattered was one more successful trip around the base paths measured out on our green, infield-like living room carpet. First base was cleverly masquerading as a

I couldn't help but wish I could run to Sam's world and take cover, even for just a little while.

magazine rack by the window, while second was safely hidden behind the leather couch that doubled as the center field fence. Third base, obviously an afterthought, was only a few steps from second and close enough to home plate that a five-year-old could make it in one leap. As my mind jumped sporadically between the contrasting images filling my living room, I couldn't help but wish I could run to Sam's world and take cover, even for just a little while. To him, every hit was a home run and every run was a game winner. He never counted the strikes or the innings played, and every game ended with a celebration. I told myself it wasn't the innocence I craved, but the courage to swing for the fence on every pitch with the confidence that it's within reach. After all, that's one of the great things about being a kid. Worlds change, but the game doesn't. Or does it?

Something happens along the way. Somewhere between Virginia Tech and my living room, somewhere between second base and home, the realities of life settle in and compromise the "what ifs" of our lives. We become all too aware that we didn't hit the ball as far as we wanted and that we're not nearly the runners we thought. We're not even sure how we made it past first with so little ability. The worst part is the nagging fear that we are the only ones who feel this way.

If you're like me, everywhere you turn, there's some tall, self-confident, perfectly coiffed, Kodak-smiling salesman or preacher telling us that with enough faith, we can accomplish anything. But they can't possibly understand what it's like where we live. How can we hope to make an eternal difference in our world when we're not even the best singer in our choir or the best Sunday school teacher in our church?

And yet, God speaks! Sometimes it's just a whisper. My wife, Cindi, has been known to suggest that God is really yelling at me; I've just lost so much hearing through the years that I think it's a whisper. Other times God speaks through silence. You've been there, haven't you? You pray and wait, then wait some more only to look around and see how God was speaking all the time. Then there are those times when God's voice is thunderous and it seems like he actually *is* yelling. For those of us who live in the shadow of insecurity, these can be the toughest times to deal with. It's almost like God's version of Newton's law of gravity. For every call there is an equal response expected. But more than the response, I fear exposing how weak I am.

Not only does God speak, but he reminds us that we have been chosen to be part of something bigger than we can imagine—something beyond what we could accomplish in our own strength. If I were to make a top ten list of my "heroes of the insecure," Gideon would surely be in the top two or three. In fact, I'd like to think he and I could have been friends. Maybe he would have confided in me what it felt like to hide from the Midianites. I could have told him how scared I was the first Sunday I directed the choir at church. We might have swapped stories of sacred encounters with a holy God. I could have told him about how God answered our twelve years of praying for a baby, and I would have loved to have heard his account of the visit from the angels. I probably would have said, "C'mon, Gideon, this is me. Angels? You? Yeah, right. You're going to deliver Israel! You're as insecure as I am. Somebody's playing the ultimate practical joke on you!"

The truth is, Gideon was a lot like me. I love his vulnerability in Judges 6:15 when he said, "O my Lord, how can I save Israel? Indeed my clan is the weakest in Manasseh, and I am the least in my father's house" (NKJV). Here's a man who spent his days separating the chaff from the straw, yet God sees something in Gideon. If you remember the story, you know that Gideon's battle strategy wasn't exactly impressive. He and his small army came in and made a bunch of noise in the middle of the night, and scared the Midianites enough that they all ran away. What I love most about the story is how God took Gideon's fear and transformed it into the very weapon he used against the enemy.

The scriptures bring us story after story after story of how God is able to use our weaknesses for his good; in fact, I would go so far as to say I think he enjoys it. He let a band of trumpet players conquer the city of Jericho and a boy with stones and a sling level a mighty warrior named Goliath. Gideon laid out a fleece before a God who had nothing whatsoever left to prove, yet this same God still reached down and met Gideon at his level.

Even now new chapters are being written in this ongoing account of God's strength on display through our weakness. How else can I respond but with surrender? I am still not sure exactly what I bring to the battlefield, but I am confident that the voice that calls me to write is not my own. I respond to that voice with trepidation, yet with courage. Even though I can't see home plate from where I stand, God reminds me that all I have to do is keep running. After all, he chose me for the game.

TWO

Blessed Are the Weak

The LORD *protects the simple; when I was brought low,*
he saved me (Psalm 116:6).

Remember the Alamo! It was the valiant battle cry of a century past. These three simple words still evoke images of courage in the face of devastating odds. They are words sustained through legend and lore with almost sacred reverence. Even the casual historian remembers that William Barret Travis and his band of weary insurgents who defended the mission-turned-fortress paid the ultimate price. While death was neither the goal nor the expectation, it was a risk dutifully embraced by those who believed in a cause bigger than themselves. They were heroes whose story has been reduced to three simple words: Remember the Alamo!

One of the central pieces of the Alamo story also seems to be the one most often forgotten. Those who stayed to defend the mission lost their lives in the process. Even the few men who survived the battle were taken before Mexican General Santa Anna where they were executed.

It was forty-six days after the fall of the Alamo when General Sam Houston, still riding the wave of anger, decided it was time to act. To the chorus of "Remember the Alamo," he and his small army of volunteers mounted a surprise attack at San Jacinto. History records a victory so decisive it led to Santa Anna's capture and the path to freedom for Texas.

On May 1, 2010, a century and a half after the bloody siege of 1836, I went to San Antonio for some meetings. They ended earlier than expected, allowing me time to take in the beauty of the downtown River Walk. The memory remains fresh because of the conflicting emotions that wrestled for my attention on that particular Saturday afternoon. As I sat barely three blocks from the place where history still hovered in the humid south Texas air, I thought about healing. Not just any healing: *my* healing. It had been twenty years to the day since God had leaned down and whispered peace to my diseased throat tissue. Each year on May 1, Cindi and I mark the mostly private anniversary with a dinner of thanksgiving. After living so many years in which the simple act of swallowing required special graces, eating always seemed the most proper way to celebrate our miracle. As each year passed, the anniversaries as well as the celebrations became more significant. If I had to be out of town, we would not cancel, but merely delay the dinner till I got home.

The endless parade of strangers seemed the perfect contrast to the serenity of the river as they both wound their way past the outdoor café where I sat. While the red umbrella above my table offered a temporary reprieve from the noonday sun, I took advantage of the moment to call home. I could tell from Cindi's "Hello" that something wasn't right. After nearly thirty years of marriage, you begin to get a feel for those kinds of things. Before I could even ask, the answer came. "It's raining," she said. "Raining hard." Since our conversations seldom included weather conditions, I assumed there was more to the story. She said there was something different about this rain. It was falling harder than she had ever seen, and she worried the ground couldn't hold it much longer. The creek beside the house was rising too quickly and the kids were getting anxious.

Since Nashville had never flooded that I was aware of, I tried to reassure her that it would probably let up soon and that I would be home in a day. As it turned out, I would be wrong on both counts. By the time I got back to the hotel, I turned on the television only to find that pictures of my neighborhood had already become the lead story in the national news. I listened intently as phrases like *one hundred-year flood . . . homes evacuated . . . airport closed . . .* brought my feelings of helplessness front and center.

Longfellow wrote, "The best thing one can do when it is raining is to let it rain," but it wasn't that easy. As I watched and waited a thousand miles from where the clouds gathered, I felt the weight of the storm begin to engulf me as well. It was as if all my worries, my uncertainties, and even my lack of faith were exposed, and for the first time ever I was forced to confront what I had long suspected: In spite of all the evidence to the contrary, I was a weak man.

There—I said it! The secret, long sequestered behind walls of pride, had been exposed. The fortress had been penetrated. My Alamo moment had come, and though I had not surrendered, I felt defeated nonetheless. Where was the euphoric sense of peace that was supposed to result from such an admission? Where was the refuge of Psalm 61? The strong tower against the foe? It was not enough to know God could hear *me*. I desperately needed to hear *him*.

If there is a positive aspect to finding yourself alone in crisis moments, it is that God has better access to your attention. In the second-floor sanctuary of a Best Western hotel room, God began to speak with deafening clarity, and his self-acknowledged child of weakness—whether out of fear or faith—began to listen.

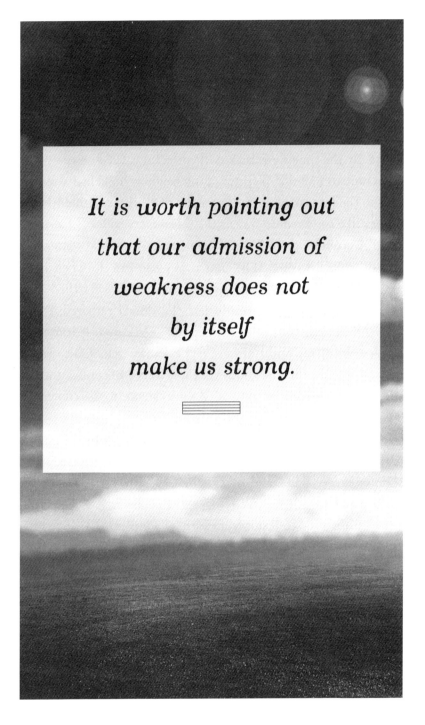

It is worth pointing out
that our admission of
weakness does not
by itself
make us strong.

On a day when I should have been overwhelmed with gratitude for the blessing of healing, I had settled for being absorbed with my own selfish wish list. How thankless I must have seemed with all my whining and worrying over things that were never in my control or out of his to begin with. As much as I wanted to go home, the biggest issue for me was to know that Cindi and the kids were safe. Since that was never really in question, I would simply wait for the water to subside. I didn't realize that my unexpected solitude would help me see my weakness for the blessing it really was.

In one of the great paradoxes of the faith, Paul wrote to the Corinthians that when we are weak, we are strong. Had I claimed that truth as my own? At best, I was still a work in progress. I could have attributed the blame to a lifetime of low self-esteem issues or misguided humility, but that wouldn't have solved anything. Since I had already come clean with my weakness, the moment seemed right to begin to live in the strength.

It is worth pointing out that our admission of weakness does not by itself make us strong. It does, however, give us a better vantage point to identify the true source of strength. In Paul's letter to the Romans, he writes that God's eternal power and divine nature have been on display in creation itself. Translation: Gaze at a mountain or take in the auburn shades of a sunset; wade barefoot in the ocean or count some stars. Then tell me how mighty you think you are. It's all about perspective.

I suspect it was a similar vantage point that led Paul to pronounce to the Philippians, "I can do all things through Christ who strengthens me" (4:13, NKJV). Paul was not attempting to use weakness as an excuse for his personal insecurities, nor did he view his weakness as a cause for celebration. It is this declaration of dependency that clears the way for God to be God in our lives, complete with signs, wonders, and even rainstorms.

Much like the story of the Alamo, my victory was not immediate or easily recognizable. By the time I was finally able to return home, the city I found was not the same as the one had I left. But then again, I was different too. While nearly every house in our neighborhood had sustained some damage, ours was untouched. The creek I had worried so much about had absorbed the impact of the water by acting as a moat and protecting the ones I loved.

For me, that journey was a beginning. In the dark of the storm I had experienced a light of revelation—a new perspective dividing the temporary from the permanent. I was marked by the Spirit of Christ and transformed by the encounter. Yes, I am weak, but I have withstood the rain and am learning what it means to live in the power of my weakness.

THREE

"Stand Up"

The Lord said to Joshua, "Stand up!
Why have you fallen upon your face?" (Joshua 7:10).

In my ongoing quest to be a more relevant father, I try to avoid making any statements beginning with the phrase, "Back when I was in school . . ." But every now and then I am convinced that my self-imposed moratorium on reminiscing is trumped by a great story. The most recent example of this was a conversation about high school marching bands. Now, I am the first to admit my lack of insight when it comes to math and science, but marching band is another story entirely. In fact, just the mention of marching band is enough to incite a full reenactment of the glorious Friday nights spent between the sidelines at Western High School in Parma, Michigan. I was a fearless young trumpet player, braving the bitter elements even as the frozen mouthpiece rattled against my teeth in cadence with the school fight song:

Western High School, hats off to thee.
To our colors, true we shall ever be . . .

I think you get the picture. If you were never blessed to be a part of the elite society known as marching band, there are some things you should know. First of all, marching band is not a one- or two-year deal. Once you're in, it will follow you the rest of your life. Anyone who has ever donned the white gloves and feather plume will forever feel compelled to stand tall at the mere sound of anything resembling John Philip Sousa. The practices are intense and pride goes deep. It can be more consuming than any sport and can only be fully appreciated by those who themselves are former marchers.

In the interest of full disclosure, I freely admit that as a freshman, playing all the notes was not a priority. I decided early on that the upperclassmen could carry the musical responsibilities while I set my sights on mastering the difficult task of marching in formation. It was only when I reached my sophomore year that I realized that every trumpet player's goal during marching season was simply to play as loud as possible—no finesse required. Ten steps forward, five steps to the left. Back straight, trumpet parallel to the ground. I knew I was part of a special design even though I couldn't see it from where I was. Success was measured by knowing I was exactly where I was supposed to be on a given note. It was only years later when I visited my old high school for a football game that I was able to see how the formation spelled out the letters WHS on the field.

These are the images that come to mind when I read about the marching band in the Old Testament and the man who led them. In one of the more famous battles in Scripture I can almost see Joshua as drum major, calling out the drill just as the Lord had drawn it up. The formation itself was not a difficult one—in fact, all the Israelites had to do was march in a big circle around the walls of Jericho. Nothing too fancy about that.

That is the story of Joshua—right? We not only know it by memory—most of us can sing it. All together now: "Joshua fit de battle of Jericho and the walls came a-tumblin' down." While I love the visual of the victorious march complete with the ark of the covenant and priests blowing horns, there is more to the man and to the story than just tumblin' walls.

So what do we really know about Joshua? I asked that very question of a retired minister friend of mine and he said, "Well, we do know he was an orphan." I told him I must have missed that piece of the story and asked how he came to that conclusion. He responded with, "Well, Scriptures tell us he was the son of Nun." (Insert groans here!)

Old jokes from retired preachers aside, we do know that Joshua was the chosen successor to Moses, leader of Israel, fighter of battles, conquering hero, and obedient servant of the Lord. Not a bad résumé. It's no wonder that God could use him in such mighty ways. With all these well-documented examples of Joshua's faithfulness and military successes, why, then, am I drawn to a lesser-known encounter between this august defender of the faith and his sovereign God?

In Joshua 7:6, we find Joshua facedown before the ark of the Lord. It wasn't just a quick, gratuitous bending of the knee. I'm not sure what time of day he started, but we know he stayed there until the evening. Now bear in mind Joshua wasn't the first or the last to fall prostrate before God. When Ezekiel saw the presence of the Lord, he fell. The same thing happened with Daniel, Paul, and even the apostle John. In fact, this wasn't even the first time for Joshua. Just two chapters earlier he was in the same position, but with a different motivation and a different response from God. As Joshua found out, a lot can change in two chapters.

In chapter 5, Joshua was strong and courageous. Morale was high among the Israelites. They had pledged their allegiance to

Joshua as they had to Moses before him. God had already parted the Jordan River and promised them the city of Jericho. Things were good. It is no wonder Joshua fell on his face and worshiped. What was God's response? In verse 15, "The commander of the army of the Lord said to Joshua, 'Remove the sandals from your feet, for the place where you stand is holy.'" And of course, he did.

Over the next two chapters Joshua faced two different battles with two different results. One was a resounding victory, the other a demoralizing setback. The jubilation of watching Jericho's walls collapse was tempered by the thirty-six lives lost in the battle for Ai. In chapter 7, Joshua once again fell before the Lord, eye to eye with the fertile soil of the Jordan Valley. But this time, everything was different. What a sight it must have been to watch this once-venerable leader cowering in self-pity and humiliation. The torn garment and the dust on his head were painful displays of mourning in the presence of a disheartened people and a merciful God.

Here's what the Lord could have said: "Joshua! Do you not remember all that we have been through? When you defeated the Amalekites in battle, I walked beside you. I stood with you as Moses passed down the mantle of leadership. I crossed the Jordan before you and allowed Jericho's fortress to fall without a drop of blood. After all we have been through, do you really think I would abandon you this quickly? The land of promise is not yet in your grasp. The best is yet to come."

While this response may have been proper and even justified, the Lord instead commanded, "Stand up!" Were these words of reproach or reprimand? Possibly, but that is not how I read it. I think it was more of a "Stand up! Put on your big boy pants and get back to what I called you to." "Stand up! Tune up the band. You haven't gotten to the best song yet." "Stand up! Yes, you are in the land, but it is not yours yet." "Stand up! There are battles yet to fight and cities yet to fall." "Stand up! Walk with me in the surrender of obedience and know that I am God."

It seems no matter how many times I read this story, the words of centuries past seem to fall on me with the freshness of the morning dew. The same voice that called to Joshua seeks us out and finds us in our weakness. The command is simple and straightforward: "Stand up!" How can we hope to see tomorrow's promise when we are facedown in today's despair? Look around and tell me what you see. How many Jordan Rivers and Red Sea moments will it take before we really trust him? If we expect the walls surrounding us to come tumblin' down, maybe—just maybe—the Lord is waiting on us to stand up and start marching.

And so I do. The fearless trumpet player takes his place in the formation once again. Success is measured by knowing I am exactly where I am supposed to be. I know I am part of a special design even though I can't see it from where I am. I am marching to a strangely familiar cadence, for I have heard the song before.

Where He leads me I will follow,
Where He leads me I will follow,
Where He leads me I will follow,
I'll go with Him, with Him all the way.

—E. W. Blandly, Nineteenth-century Salvation Army officer

FOUR

"Kneel Down"

But if we hope for what we do not see, we wait for it with patience.
Likewise the Spirit helps us in our weakness; for we do not know
how to pray as we ought, but that very Spirit intercedes
with sighs too deep for words (Romans 8:25-26).

"**If you** could be any superhero you wanted, which one would you choose?" Even though somewhat disarmed by the question, I knew the earnestness of his inquiry demanded an honest response. "Well, Sam, I would have to think about that one for a while," I replied. In actuality, my mind immediately went to one of the all-time greatest superheroes, but one I knew Sam was way too young to remember.

Of course, I'm talking about Underdog. For those of you who either cannot remember that far back or are in denial about your age, let me tell you about him. Underdog was one of a long line of anthropomorphic Saturday morning cartoon characters from the mid-'60s. His secret identity was the mild-mannered Shoeshine Boy who could take an energy pill from his secret compartment ring and transform himself into the fearless crime-fighter and vanquisher of evil known as Underdog.

The animation was unsophisticated and predictable and the story line seldom changed. His enemies had names like Riff Raff and Simon Bar Sinister, and every episode included at least one daring yet successful rescue of Sweet Polly Purebred. I decided early on that Sweet Polly was either very unlucky or not very smart because she always found herself in perilous situations.

You may be wondering why I would decide on Underdog over some of the obvious choices like Batman or Superman. After all, Underdog was not tall or muscular and was unassuming at best. He was so short that his blue cape hung down well past his feet. Even his voice seemed to lack the presence of a true superhero. In theory, as a wannabe songwriter, the fact that all his lines were delivered in rhymes would have been sufficient reason for me to identify with him. I could have even gone so far as to put a spiritual spin on the lyrics of the theme song:

> *When in this world the headlines read*
> *Of those whose hearts are filled with greed*
> *Who rob and steal from those who need*
> *To right this wrong with blinding speed*
> *Goes Underdog! Underdog! Underdog! Underdog!*[1]
>
> —W. Watts Biggers

But none of those reasons tell the entire story. Although the answer divulges considerably more about me than it does about Underdog, I suppose that after all these years, a little confession is good for the soul. The real story is this: of all the superheroes that filled the Saturday morning TV screen, Underdog was the only one I felt like I could really relate to. I was small for my age and always seemed to lack self-confidence, even in a home where I was showered with love in abundance.

And so it went each Saturday morning. For thirty minutes reality was suspended as I watched someone with the same shortcomings as me do what I could never do—take on sinister forces, calm rebellion, rescue those in distress, and do it all with the greatest of ease. After all, isn't that what we want from our superheroes?

One of my early real-life influences was a man named Bob Benson who, much like Underdog, always seemed to break the stereotype of a hero. He possessed the unique ability to write and speak in understated tones that left both readers and listeners feeling like they had just shared a cup of coffee with him in his living room. Bob was my Sunday school teacher when I first moved to Nashville, and along with his brother John, ran one of the industry's largest Christian record labels and publishing companies. Even though cancer would take him before I got to glean as much wisdom from him as I wanted, his impact on me was profound and long-lasting.

Even as a young teenager I can remember struggling not so much with the question of whether God had called me—that was never in question—but with why God would call me, yet not bless me with the gifts I would need to accomplish the work. To this day I have no doubts that God allowed me to learn from one who refused to be defined by inabilities and weaknesses, but instead, impacted the kingdom through them. That was who I wanted to be then and still aspire to be now.

To the best of my memory, I was never one of those kids who tied a homemade cape around my neck and pretended to fly, but that did not preclude me from spending my share of time living in the land of "what if." My villains may have seemed imaginary to some, but the battle they waged against me was persistent and unyielding—the fear of not being chosen for the team, the unrelenting health struggles, the longing to have a friend, and the challenge of being one. If there ever was someone who needed a superhero, it was me.

The discouraging reality is that if left unattended, the weakness of our youth will pursue us into adulthood where the sense of hopelessness is only magnified. And no matter what the age, it is impossible to conquer real-life obstacles with make-believe solutions. After all, Saturday morning's heroes are no equal for Sunday morning's problems.

The good news is this: We are not a people left to rely on our own strength, and our weakness does not have the final say in who and what we become. Scripture is full of reminders that we do not face our battles alone. In Isaiah 26, "the LORD JEHOVAH is [our] everlasting strength" (v. 4, KJV). In Isaiah 40, God "gives strength to the weary and increases the power of the weak" (v. 29, NIV). In Philippians 4, we can do "everything through Christ, who gives [us] strength" (v. 13, NLT). And the list goes on.

In the midst of these myriad assurances, there is one passage in particular that has always intrigued me. In his letter to the Romans, Paul wrote, "Likewise the Spirit helps us in our weakness; for we do not know how to pray as we ought, but that very Spirit intercedes with sighs too deep for words" (Romans 8:26).

My suspicion is that all too often we read the first part of this text as if it's saying the Spirit will help us when we are feeling weak. That is true, but such a limited interpretation severely undercuts the broader intent of Paul's words. What he is really saying is that we are weak. Period. It is not a temporary condition that rises and falls like the ocean's tide—it is who we are by our very nature. We are a weak people.

Interestingly enough, Paul does not stop there, but goes on to build a curious bridge between our ongoing infirmities and the power of prayer. While the narrative of weakness is certainly not a new one for him, this verse sheds new light on the Holy Spirit's role. By tethering our helplessness to our petitions, Paul offers a

"Likewise the Spirit helps us in our weakness; for we do not know how to pray as we ought, but that very Spirit intercedes with sighs too deep for words" (Romans 8:26).

definitive perspective of God's sovereign power and the Spirit's ability to move in the balance.

Let me try and say it another way: I think Paul is making the point that our problem is not just one of weakness, but one of prayer. The more we understand about how we are to pray and who we are praying to, the more we recognize the essential nature and sheer splendor of the Spirit's intercession.

If I were to ask you where you stand on the matter of prayer, I would imagine almost anyone reading this book would testify about the power of prayer in their life. Even a novice preacher could fill a month's worth of Sundays on the topic. After all, prayer is one of the biggest issues for all believers, no matter what their faith. Muslims pray to Allah, Buddhists to Buddha, and I suspect even the agnostic occasionally says something to someone out there. The question then becomes, what distinguishes our prayers from those of other beliefs? I could say that I am a changed person when I am praying, but even the Hindus chanting their mantras to Brahman would claim to find themselves more at peace as a result of their prayers. There has to be something more substantial—something more definitive.

I would suggest that the correct response is found front and center in Paul's reassurance to the Romans. We have an intermediary One who appeals on our behalf in the midst of our helplessness. First Corinthians 2:11 declares "no one comprehends what is truly God's except the Spirit of God." Who better, then, to intercede to God on our behalf than the same Spirit who searches and knows our hearts?

Martin Luther once prayed, "Grant that I may not pray alone with the mouth; help me that I may pray from the depths of my heart." He was referring to what Scripture calls "groaning"—a term interspersed throughout Scripture from creation to the cross to illustrate that deep, agonizing cry that reaches all the way to God's ears. When the depths of our petitions exceed even our words, one of the high-water marks of faith is revealed in the absolute helplessness of our humanness. If we back up to Romans 8:17-18, we see the link between our suffering and God's glory. Our weakness for his power—not a bad trade-off, wouldn't you say? I believe that is part of what makes this passage so profound—to think there are times when our anguish is so intense that even the Spirit groans on our behalf.

All of that sounds great, but are we really allowing it to affect how we pray? According to James 5, "the prayers of someone who is a righteous person have God's full attention" (translation mine). The sad truth is that most of the time I just don't feel all that righteous, and no matter how fervently I approach the throne, I still don't feel like I get it right. In those times when the problem eclipses the promise, I take consolation in knowing that even when I am overwhelmed by weakness to the point of silence, my petitions are still heard. I have an Advocate who knows my heart and touches God on my behalf. The Spirit appears in the midst of my distress as if my own personal superhero were doing what I cannot do on my own—fighting my battles with a strength greater than my own. These are battles that should never have been fought with—and cannot be won with—my armaments alone. The Spirit groans; God listens; change happens—no cape needed.

FIVE

"Living in the Vapor"

For we do not have a high priest who is unable to sympathize with our weaknesses, but we have one who in every respect has been tested as we are, yet without sin. Let us therefore approach the throne of grace with boldness, so that we may receive mercy and find grace to help in time of need (Hebrews 4:15-16).

Before we took our seats in the auditorium, my mind was already nearly overflowing with memories—memories of Allison starting school. I thought about her first day of kindergarten. The kindergartners only attended school a half day for the first few weeks in order to help them (translation: help the parents) ease their way into the new routine. We pulled up bright and early on that Tuesday morning in front of the brick building of chalkboards and hallways, parked the car, and headed inside. I was trying to be strong for Allison's sake, but I don't think I was fooling her at all.

She grabbed my hand and held on tight as we made our way through the double glass doors, past the office, down the hall to the right and then down another hall to the right. When we finally reached the door with Miss Parker's name on it, I knelt down, still holding Allison's tiny hand, and prayed that God would help her in this new beginning. After praying, we walked into the classroom and found the desk with her name on it. Only then did she reluctantly let go of my hand.

Call it another evidence of my weak nature, but I cried all the way back to the car, drove home, and sat and looked at the clock until I could go back and pick her up again. If day two was supposed to be easier, no one had notified my heart. We repeated the routine from the parking lot to the hallway. The only difference on day two was that she let go of my hand as we reached the door rather than waiting until we found her desk. I kissed her good-bye and headed home to once again watch the clock.

On day three, I was starting to see a pattern. On this day she let go of my hand as we walked through the front door, and I followed her lead past the office, down the hall to the right, and then down another hall to the right. She seemed to know where she was going and my hand was no longer as necessary as it had been only two days earlier. I was still not prepared for her words on day four as we pulled up to the school, when she looked up and said, "You can let me out here, Dad." I told her if it was okay, now *I* was the one who needed to hold *her* hand.

It was not by accident that those memories seemed so fresh in my mind that particular night. Because Allison was only in eighth grade, I saw no reason to approach the impending high school orientation meeting with any real sense of apprehension. Like many of the other unsuspecting first-timers, I came fully anticipating a list of guidelines, a pep talk from the new principal, and maybe even a walk-through of the campus. What I did not expect was to be greeted at the door with a barrage of college brochures, ACT testing information, and material on how to apply for scholarships. I personally would have been better served had they provided therapists trained in dealing with posttraumatic parenting disorder. While I am quite certain the next two hours of speeches and media presentations were filled with worthwhile and timely information, I honestly can't remember any of it. For me it was all too much, too soon.

A few rows over I saw Jeff and Kim. Behind them were Tina and Robin and a few other close friends whose paths might have never crossed with ours were it not for our daughters. I was struck by how many moments we had all shared in the years since kindergarten first brought us together. Friendships forged at field days, fund-raisers, and class parties—and now—high school. I wondered if they too felt blindsided by the speed at which time had passed—or was it just me?

The evening concluded with assurances from the principal, someone I had never met before, telling us we had nothing to fear. He claimed to know exactly how we felt and boldly declared that he could be trusted with the next chapter in our children's lives. But I wasn't buying it—at least not yet. My struggle was not one of trust, but readiness—and not Allison's readiness, but mine. The issue was not whether they could sufficiently equip her, but whether I could bring myself to step aside and allow it to happen—as if this were a choice that was mine to make anyway.

The memories continued to consume me. I thought back to the first time we left her in the church nursery, how I peered anxiously through the small window in the door until the workers gave me a not-so-gentle request to leave. She was barely two weeks into kindergarten when they informed me I could no longer walk her to class. I was the dad in the car following the bus on field trips and the first one in line to pick her up from elementary school at the end of the day. And even now, all these years later, I am struck by how little has changed. Everywhere I turn, something or someone is forcing me to let go before I am ready.

I have always been convinced that God had a hidden agenda when he brought my wife, Cindi, into my life. It was his way of providing calm to my chaos and stability to my restlessness. She is the math teacher and I the poet. She sees the world in black and white while I am drawn to the abstract. The kids go to her for help with homework and to me when they want ice cream for breakfast. It is not so much oil and water as what the Greek philosopher Heraclitus called the *unity of opposites*—two vantage points of the same goal.

It should have come as no surprise, then, that her take on the evening's events was profoundly different from mine. The dialogue on the short ride back to the house was mostly one-sided, with me doing the majority of the listening. Had I not known better, I would have sworn she had been at a different meeting than I had. Without even a trace of angst in her voice, she talked with excitement about watching Allison grow up so well and knowing she was as ready as she could be for the days ahead.

There are but two constants in this story of life. We are born and we die, we and do not control the timing of either. James 4:14 refers to life as "a vapor that appears for a little time and then vanishes away" (NKJV). How we cultivate this vapor has both immediate and eternal consequences. I have lived long enough to get a sense of how short life really is. Even though the story line can be broken down into chapters and verses, the narrative will almost certainly be defined by how we live within the parentheses—in those seldom-seen pockets of life where faith is tested, choices made, and character defined.

In 1 Chronicles 29:28, we read that King David died "in a good old age, full of days, riches, and honor." If we could each write our own exit papers, I think you would agree that David's is about as good as it gets. Unfortunately, real life seldom plays out that way. We can live an honorable life, yet never have honor bestowed upon us. We can work tirelessly and still fail to achieve riches. We all know of way too many scenarios in which someone left before his or her days were full. I find it somewhat ironic that this same King David more than once in the Psalms asked God to reveal to him the number of his days. And why? That God would remind him just how frail life really is.

While even in the most hypothetical of scenarios I would not choose to know the number of my days, I accept the fact that a vapor, by its very nature, is temporary. We are not here for long. It has always seemed a bit peculiar to me how we light candles on a cake to celebrate what we too often fear—the passage of time. We sing and laugh even as the breath of life is used to extinguish the flame. The smoke dissipates as a vapor, and God reveals himself in the metaphor. Fortunately, the lesson does not fall on deaf ears.

Although I do not enjoy the aging process, neither do I fear it like I once did. The weaker part of my nature does, however, question whether I am a worthy steward of the days I have been given. From the time I was young, I have felt both challenged and guilty at times when reading Luke 12:48, which says that "to whom much has been given, much will be required." I found myself living in the contradiction of feeling that I didn't have enough to offer, yet was not doing nearly enough with what I had.

Several years ago, a pastor friend asked me what my life verse was. If you are not familiar with that phrase, it is usually a Bible verse that has specifically challenged, changed, motivated, or defined someone. I replied that I had one, but I doubted he would want to hear it. After a few minutes of coaxing, I told him that my life verse was from an old country song by Larry Gatlin called "I'm Standing Here Trying to Matter." While I am still not entirely certain what I may have to offer, I am intent on using those gifts with passion and purpose in the kingdom of God.

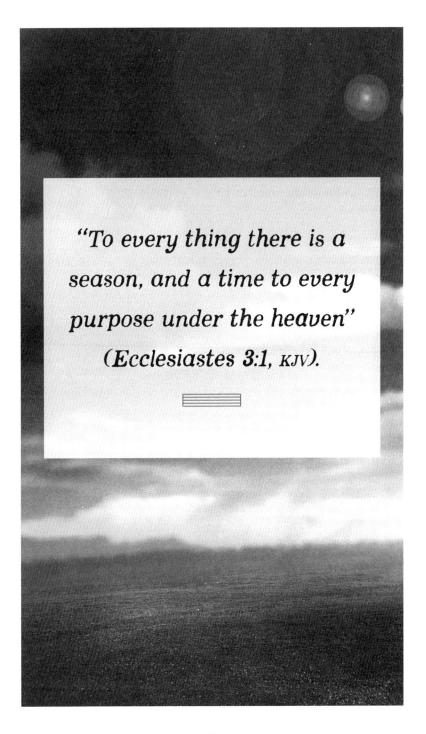

"To every thing there is a season, and a time to every purpose under the heaven" (*Ecclesiastes 3:1, KJV*).

I think about the country song from a few years back that encouraged us to live like we were dying. It was a stirring account of how a terminally ill patient chose to spend his final days. Even as I wonder what I should aim to accomplish, I am more concerned with the fact that all too often, it takes a brush with Jordan for us to embrace the sacredness of time.

When the passage of time finds its way into the discussion, someone will invariably inject portions of Ecclesiastes 3 into the conversation—as if knowing there is a season for everything should make us feel better about gray hair, diminished hearing, and bifocals. The sad part is that in most cases, they conclude with verse 8 when the truth I think most of us need to hear does not begin until verse 10. In case it is unfamiliar, I will give it to you here:

> I have seen the business that God has given to everyone to be busy with. He has made everything suitable for its time; moreover he has put a sense of past and future into their minds, yet they cannot find out what God has done from the beginning to the end. I know that there is nothing better for them than to be happy and enjoy themselves as long as they live; moreover, it is God's gift that all should eat and drink and take pleasure in all their toil. I know that whatever God does endures forever; nothing can be added to it, nor anything taken from it; God has done this, so that all should stand in awe before him. That which is, already has been; that which is to be, already is; and God seeks out what has gone by. (Ecclesiastes 3:10-15)

This passage is not so much a road map on how to die as much as enlightenment on how to live. And so we breathe deep and armor well, measure the costs, and minimize the risks. We gather up life's moments like buttercups from the soil, embracing each day as a gift. By choosing to confront the brevity of life rather than renounce it, we can celebrate the moments rather than fear them. Great advice, wouldn't you say? Especially for a guy learning to be the dad of a daughter going to high school.

SIX

Mountaintop Experiences

I am about to do a new thing; now it springs forth,
do you not perceive it? I will make a way in the wilderness
and rivers in the desert (Isaiah 43:19).

It was a morning I will never forget. The sun was still several hours from shining as I made my way up the winding road from the tiny village of Estes Park, Colorado, to the summit of Rocky Mountain State Park. It was my twentieth consecutive summer teaching at a conference at the YMCA campgrounds, and for nineteen of those years, I had steadfastly declared my intent to one day film a sunrise from atop the snow-laden peaks that surrounded us.

Since I have never been a huge fan of mountainous roads with no guardrails even in the daytime, I knew it would require special courage to manage the drive by myself in total darkness. When the day of now-or-never arrived, I still felt some consternation. I have to admit that what sounded like a great thing when describing it to friends in the daylight was not nearly as compelling when the alarm sounded at 4:00 that morning. I contemplated rolling over and going back to sleep because, after all, sunrises are free and there would always be another one tomorrow. In the end, I determined adventure would take precedence over risk. I grabbed my camera and tripod and set out for the mountain.

After finding what I perceived to be a worthy vantage point for a perfect sunrise, I turned off the engine and began the tedious wait for daybreak. I'm not sure a night was ever darker or more silent. With the stars casting the only light for what seemed like miles in every direction, you can imagine the panic I felt when I sensed a pair of eyes staring at me from outside my car. Turning the headlights back on, I'm still not sure who was more scared—me or the bighorn sheep whose face was pressed against my window. I will just say that I was more than ready for the sun when it finally showed its face.

Even though I have always maintained that sunsets get all the good press, what I saw in the ensuing first light was more breathtaking than anything I could have ever dreamed, and certainly more than an amateur videographer's lens could capture. I got out of the car and with camera and tripod in tow, walked to the edge of the cliff, pushed the red button on the camera, and watched and waited as God did what God does. Even as I lingered in the glory of the Father's handiwork from twelve thousand feet, I could hardly have imagined that he was saving something even more special for me that morning.

After the sun had settled on its morning destination, I walked back to the car with a sense of accomplishment and began my descent down the mountain. As I drove, I noticed something peculiar out my window. It looked as if a fine layer of crimson mist was beginning to gather in the thin morning air. Though I was unsure of what I was witnessing, my instincts told me to pull onto the narrow shoulder and get the camera out once again. If God had something else for me to see, I was determined not to miss it. As I watched through the small glass of my camera lens, the red particles began to cling together, suspended in the atmosphere to form a substance unlike anything I had ever seen before.

Even though I could not explain what was happening from a scientific standpoint, I celebrated the fact that in the stillness of the Colorado morning, God had granted me a front-row seat to the spectacular. What remained of my morning excursion was awestruck silence as I tried to reconcile the events I had experienced. What I could not have realized then was that God was not quite finished with me. He still had one more surprise left.

The dark clouds and torrential rain seemed to come out of nowhere as I continued my trek down the mountain. Because storms were not particularly uncommon for that time of day in that altitude, I didn't think much of it at first. After all, I had plenty on my mind already. As if on cue, the showers began to subside as I pulled into the parking lot of the cabin where I was staying. It was only then, as I got out of my car and looked up to where I had watched the sunrise an hour earlier, that I got a sense of what God was trying to teach me. Reaching across the heavens in all its splendor was the most brilliant rainbow I had ever seen. In the red mist of the morning, God had allowed me to see the rainbow before I ever saw the rain.

In the years since then, my mind has returned again and again to my mountaintop experience. To think what I would have missed had I stayed in my comfortable room that morning! Instead, the pursuit of what I thought I would see allowed me to experience what I could have never dreamed.

In the same way, I am convinced something significant happens when we begin to seek the will of a God we cannot understand, a God we cannot reason, a God we cannot hold in our hand. There has always been a bit of a disconnect for me in how often we claim God to be, as Paul wrote, One "that is able to do exceeding abundantly above all that we ask or think" (Ephesians

3:20, KJV), yet everything in us wants to understand what God is up to and why. The simple truth is that it is impossible for God to do what is beyond our understanding until we are willing to surrender our need to understand.

I love the old country song recorded by Ronnie Milsap back in the mid-'70s that said, "I've got 20/20 vision but only looking back." Isn't that the way it is sometimes in our relationship with God? We look back and see how he was at work orchestrating the pieces of our life, even though we couldn't see it at the time.

Is it just me, or are there times in life when it would seem so much easier if God would let you take a sneak peek at tomorrow? After all, if you knew where the job was going to come from or what the results of the x-rays would reveal, can you imagine what it would do for your level of confidence? You could walk more boldly in your faith knowing that God was already at work in the details of your life.

The problem is, that would not be walking by faith at all. It would simply be trusting in our own knowledge. I love how *The Message* paraphrase of Proverbs 3:5-6 puts it: "Trust GOD from the bottom of your heart; don't try to figure out everything on your own. Listen for GOD's voice in everything you do, everywhere you go; he's the one who will keep you on track."

God is longing to do a new thing in us and through us. But the truth is that if we want to see God work in new ways, we have to be willing to take some new steps. Have you thought about how far you are willing to go and what you are willing to risk in order to reach God's extraordinary?

I hear a lot of people in ministry talk about finding the next level and yet, in far too many cases, I fear these are the same ones who would prefer that the next level find them instead. When I was younger, we used to sing a song in church that said, "There are no boundaries or limits to what God can do." It was true then and still holds true today. God does not need to expand his imagination; we just need to trust him enough to let him expand ours. However you want to say it, it may be time to walk out on some ledges, climb out on some limbs, step out of some comfort zones, and scale some new mountains—even when you can't see the guardrails. Be willing to wait for some sunrises and, above all else, learn to expect the unexpected. We are not in this alone, and our confidence comes in knowing that he who began the work is absolutely faithful to complete it (Philippians 1:6).

SEVEN

When the Team Needs You

Like good stewards of the manifold grace of God, serve one another
with whatever gift each of you has received. Whoever speaks must
do so as one speaking the very words of God; whoever serves must do
so with the strength that God supplies, so that God may be glorified
in all things through Jesus Christ. To him belong the glory
and the power forever and ever. Amen (1 Peter 4:10-11).

When it comes to sports, anyone who has ever been to a game with me will tell you I get every dime's worth out of the ticket price. I cheer the loudest, eat the most food, boo with the most intensity, and smile all the while. I like good seats with concession stand proximity and have been known to go alone if I can't get anyone to go with me. I have been at baseball games in Detroit in April when snow was falling, and suffered in the Tennessee sun at exhibition football games. The bottom line is, I just like being at a game.

When I was younger, even though I participated in that illustrious rite of passage known as little league, I experienced the thrill of the game mostly from a wooden slat bench in the dugout. I could have blamed my lack of playing time on the fact that

I was small for my age. I could have claimed that I was every bit as good as the coach's son, who never missed an inning. The real story, however, was that as a starting pitcher, I made a pretty good second-string right fielder. Looking back now, in all my years of suiting up for the game, I don't ever recall playing for a coach who was overly concerned about my self-esteem. After all, we were there to win.

Even though it sounds a little self-centered of me, my favorite games were the ones where we had just enough players show up to field a team. Although it meant a greater chance of losing, for me it represented a greater sense of belonging. There was something about knowing the coach's expectations were lower that made me want to accomplish more. It changed everything from how I walked to the batter's box to my attitude about being relegated to right field.

I wish I had some epic, heart-stopping account of how I came to bat with the game on the line and delivered the game-winning hit, but the truth is, that never happened. What defined those games for me was not that I played that much better, but that I was better for having played. There was something significant that happened just knowing the team needed me.

The concept of teamwork in ministry is not a new one by any means. We see examples of it in the earliest pages of Scripture—from Moses and Aaron to Paul and Timothy. Even in our modern culture, teamwork is a common element found in many church strategies. When we hear it preached, it usually begins with a fresh look at 1 Corinthians 12:

> If the foot would say, "Because I am not a hand, I do not belong to the body," that would not make it any less a part of the body. And if the ear would say, "Because I am not an eye, I do not belong to the body," that would not make it any less a part of the body. If the whole body were an eye, where would

the hearing be? If the whole body were hearing, where would the sense of smell be? (Vv. 15-17)

This describes teamwork, right? People of faith united in a cause bigger than themselves. It takes you using your gift and me using my gift. And just in case you don't know what your gift is, you're in luck. We have a book for you to read and a survey you can take to determine what your spiritual gifts are. Sounds easy enough in theory.

Now don't get me wrong. I absolutely believe it is part of the church's responsibility to help its members identify their spiritual gifts. In fact, I would go so far as to say that outside of your initial salvation experience, one of the most exciting events in your spiritual life can be the moment you come to know where and how you can best serve the Body of Christ. We as the church have the privilege and the responsibility of encouraging, counseling, and supporting each other in the name of Christ.

My concern is that, should we ever become overzealous in our pursuit of specific gifts, we might overlook the one piece that makes the whole analogy work. Verse 18 of 1 Corinthians 12 says, "God arranged the members in the body, each one of them, as he chose."

"As he chose." If we neglect that crucial piece of the process, we risk ending up with a Mr. Potato Head-type implementation of the scripture. As anyone old enough to have played with this classic toy remembers, you can put an eye where the ear should go and the ear where the nose should go and so on. The result is that you end up with all the body parts in the wrong places.

So it is in the Body of Christ. We can fill all the positions in the church with this person or that person who may not be gifted for that specific job. But in the process the person *and* the church will miss out on experiencing the more excellent way Paul writes about in 1 Corinthians 12:31 and 1 Corinthians 13.

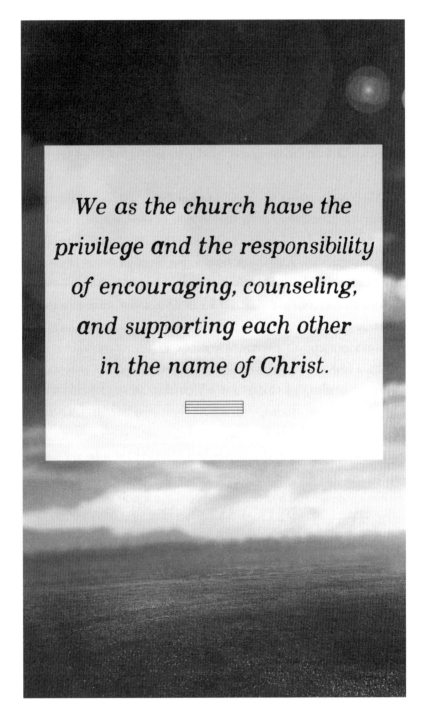

We as the church have the privilege and the responsibility of encouraging, counseling, and supporting each other in the name of Christ.

So if I, a Christ-follower, am truly seeking the will of God, the giver of all gifts, shouldn't that be the end of the discussion? I mean, someone has to play right field. Or be the ear. Or the foot. I am not convinced that it is a sign of weakness to long for skills we do not possess; more likely it is a symptom of being human. It is our very nature to be frail and insecure until we become so preoccupied with "what's next" that we miss "what is."

Perhaps, like me, you have even tried to negotiate with God about how you could use more impressive gifts to more effectively build his kingdom. Okay, maybe you haven't actually written down your list, but I suspect many people have one. I used to think things like, "Just think how much better I could preach if only God would have trusted me with a deeper voice or a more charismatic personality, " or, "If I had been taller or born a great singer, my impact on the kingdom would be so much greater." And let's not forget money. I will never forget speaking at a church a few years ago where the prelude to prayer included a corporate reading of things for which they were trusting God. The list included finding money in their mailbox and winning the lottery. And all God's people said, "Amen."

In other words, if the coach had allowed the players to fill out the lineup card, I suspect we would have had a very crowded pitcher's mound and a desolate outfield. As much as I hate to admit it, the coach knew I belonged in right field. What he needed was for me to be the best right fielder I could be. After all, it was his call to arrange the team in the order we needed.

And so it is with the Body of Christ. We are all given unique gifts and called to serve in unique ways. When we pray for God to bless us with greater gifts, or larger platforms, our focus can easily shift from his ministry to our own agenda. As hard as it is to remember at times, God has given us everything we need to achieve all that he wants to accomplish through us. The ultimate use of our gifts has always been and always will be single in its purpose. And what is that purpose? According to 1 Peter,

> Each one of you should use whatever gift you have received to serve others, as faithful stewards of God's grace in its various forms. If anyone speaks, they should do so as one who speaks the very words of God. If anyone serves, they should do so with the strength God provides, so that in all things God may be praised through Jesus Christ. To him be the glory and the power for ever and ever. Amen. (4:10-11, NIV)

After all, it's not about how much we have to offer, but whom we offer it to. The measure of success is no longer what we have accomplished, but whether God received glory through it. All of a sudden, the small Sunday school class you have taught for years goes from feeling like an obligation to an opportunity. Singing in the choir is no longer one voice in a crowd, but a sacred hallelujah lifted to the King of kings and Lord of lords.

The agonizing waiting and wondering if we will be chosen for the team has been settled. We could not be more—pitcher, catcher, even right field. In the words of the old hymn, "I'll go where you want me to go, dear Lord. / I'll be what you want me to be."

Many of us know the story of John Wesley, the founder of the Methodist Church. Back in the 1700s he published a book for the Methodists in North America and included what has come to be known as Wesley's Covenant Prayer. I cannot think of a better way to close this chapter than to offer Wesley's words as the cry of my own heart.

Wesley's Covenant Prayer

I am no longer my own, but yours.
Put me to what you will, rank me with whom you will;
put me to doing, put me to suffering.
Let me be employed by you or laid aside by you,

enabled for you or brought low by you.
Let me be full, let me be empty.
Let me have all things, let me have nothing.
I freely and heartily yield all things
to your pleasure and disposal.
And now, O glorious and blessed God,
Father, Son, and Holy Spirit,
you are mine, and I am yours. So be it.
And the covenant which I have made on earth,
let it be ratified in heaven.
Amen.

EIGHT

The Church of My Childhood

And I tell you, you are Peter, and on this rock I will build
my church, and the gates of Hades will not prevail against it
(Matthew 16:18).

If I could reverse the days and take you to the church of my childhood, you would be neither stirred by her beauty nor overwhelmed by her grandeur. Like nearly every other sanctuary built in the fifties, it was longer than it was wide and boasted very little in the way of architectural innovation. The center of the platform was graced with a hardwood pulpit that matched the pews out front as well as those in the choir loft.

In the church of my childhood, everyone carried a King James Version of the Bible and every Bible was bound with black leather. The hymnals were nested in a wooden pocket on the back of each pew, and we rarely sang a song newer than one hundred years. The only musicians needed were a pianist and organist, and those who played held the job for life. Families rode in one car, dressed in their Sunday finest, and usually sat together in the same row once they got there. Children were raised not to run in church and never would have dreamed of bringing food or drink into the sanctuary.

The preacher lived next door to the church and was the first one there on Sunday and the last one to leave. The term "pastor" garnered a sense of reverence, and a suit and tie was the customary apparel, no matter what time of the day or what day of the week.

In the church of my childhood, the story of the gospel moved the heart of an eight-year-old boy and eternity was settled at an old wooden prayer bench. Responding to God's call to ministry was the easy part. The challenge would be finding my place among the images of ministry I inherited from the church of my childhood. The images were blurred not by what I was taught, but by what I perceived. Some of those included the following:

1. The Priesthood Is Only for Pastors

No one actually said this when I was growing up, but the insinuation was definitely there. I can remember as a young believer telling someone I felt called to ministry. They responded by saying that I would make a fine pastor someday. And you know what? Maybe someday I will. But their interpretation of God's call for me seemed a lot more specific than what I was feeling at the time.

It was not uncommon in those days to hear a new convert profess a calling either to preach or to serve on the mission field. After you got past those two choices, there was not a whole lot left to choose from. You can imagine the reactions I got when I told people I felt God was calling me to be a writer. That was just not how people expected God to speak in those days. Even then I was not as interested in being a rebel with a cause as much as being faithful to a call that was uniquely and distinctly mine.

First Peter 2:9 tells us we are a chosen people and a royal priesthood. We are called by God and given access by faith, and our response is a lifetime of service. This sacred calling is more than an event we must attend; it is a lifestyle that demands our heart, soul, and mind. In my childhood, it hardly seemed plausible that a son of a factory worker and school secretary would find his place in ministry with a pen and paper. I am blessed, however, that the church of my childhood embraced a calling they may not have understood rather than try to steer me toward the more familiar road.

2. Mission Fields Are Only Faraway Lands

I'm not sure if the only missionaries that ever spoke at my childhood church were from Africa, or if those were just the ones that had the most profound effect on me. Either way, more than forty years later, I am intrigued and slightly amused that the great fear of my childhood was that a "yes" to God would put me on the fast track to Africa. The irony is that my "yes" meant God would instead call me to Nashville, Tennessee, to work in the music business. Knowing what I know now, I am convinced that any other place would have presented far fewer challenges and certainly less stress.

My wife, Cindi, while growing up as the third of four children in a Florida parsonage, felt a call to the mission field. God's voice was obvious and her response was one of obedience, even though she could not see the path that would lead her there. As the needle drifted across the time line called life, she would enroll in a Christian university, study education, accept a blind date with a fledgling songwriter, and fall for his irresistible charm and dashing good looks. (Okay, I may have embellished that last part.)

In the years ahead, she would learn an important truth about the beauty of surrender: the God of our calling is also the God of our provision. Her commitment did not ask her to relinquish her dreams—only her plans. In the years ahead, an eighth grade math class in a public school would prove to be no less a mission field than a thatched hut nestled in the Amazon rain forest.

Nearly any discussion of missions in the church of my childhood eventually found its way back to the Great Commission of Matthew 28:19: "Go therefore and make disciples of all nations." Fresh eyes on a familiar text reveal a truth too often overlooked: The phrase "all nations" may lead to a journey across the sea or just across the street. The secret is found in the word "go."

3. Talents Refer Only to Music

For better or worse, the word "talented" was a descriptor attached to me early on by the church of my childhood. I still suspect it was fueled more by my passion for music than by any exceptional ability I might have possessed. Those who bestowed such an uncomfortable moniker upon me would have been surprised to know that playing music was never necessarily my aspiration—it was just who I was. Music also provided a much-needed refuge for me as a kid who struggled with physical as well as self-confidence issues.

This is not intended to be a referendum on my abilities or anyone else's. In fact, in my experience, the word "talented" is usually only as valid as who we are being compared with. I include the topic here because I think this is another area the church can get wrong if we are not careful.

Looking back, I realize how many gifts were represented in my circle of friends. Those gifts were the result of a combination of God's blessings, genetic hand-me-downs, and, in some cases, hard work. There were some blessed with athletic ability while others excelled in academics. There were others who seemed to be born leaders. While all of these gifts could be used to build up the Body of Christ, opportunities to use musical gifts were more public and more plentiful. Because of that, I fear I may have received encouragement and confirmation that others could have used if only they had received it.

4. Giving Is Only Financial

I don't think the church of my childhood preached nearly enough on the topic of giving. When they did preach on the subject, in far too many cases it referred only to finances. While it's true that money is one of the big three that Scripture refers to when discussing giving, I fear the other two—time and talents—are often overlooked in the process.

What if, in the middle of a sermon on stewardship, I were to remind you that we have all been given more than we deserve and it's up to each of us to use it wisely? I could then go on to argue that what we do with what we have been given is a direct reflection of our priorities. I could even use guilt to point out the dangers of squandering or overextending what we have rather than giving it back to God. Depending on how effectively I made my case, the end of the sermon might very well find you reaching for your checkbook in response. But then, what if I told you that everything in the sermon was not about money, but instead was referring to time? Interchange the word "talents" and you are left with the same result.

Last week, during one of our family dinner discussions, I listened intently as my children began to reminisce about the church of their childhood. There was zero mention of music styles or how the preacher dressed. Because the sanctuary they remember doubled as a gymnasium, running in church was not an issue and their Bible of choice could be downloaded as an app.

I love that even as each generation redefines a new normal for worship, the faith of our fathers is living still and takes precedence over the church of our childhood. The good news of the gospel still moves the heart of the seeker, and the church is in good hands.

NINE

First Steps

Be strong and courageous; do not be frightened or dismayed, for the
Lord your God is with you wherever you go (Joshua 1:9).

We are, by our very nature, a people fascinated with last things.
The newspapers report what the prisoner had for his last meal.
Many still reminisce in glowing terms about the last episode
of *M*A*S*H*. Most people over the age of forty can tell you the
name of the last guest on the long-running Johnny Carson show.
(It was Bette Midler, by the way.)

Even though I count myself among those curious about last
things, I am equally fascinated by first things. I am completely
intrigued by first lines of songs or political speeches, a baby's first
words, or where the first steps were taken. Stories about my first
car have long outlived the car itself, and Cindi and I still love to
tell the story of our first blind date.

Looking back at my favorite firsts and lasts, I am struck by
how often the two categories are unwittingly connected. A new
chapter made possible only because another chapter ended. The
more spiritual explanation would be to tie every significant tran-
sition in my life to the result of fervent prayer, deep faith, and
great courage on my part. The truth is that what at times may

have appeared to be the bold initiative of a confident man was actually a terrified response to unwanted and often unexpected change. With nearly every first step I have taken, there has been a part of me that just wanted to stop and look back over my shoulder to make sure God was still behind me.

It would be so much easier if God worked off a grid. Not just any grid, but *my* grid. I could tell him when I was ready for change and, just because he loved me, he would go before me and ensure the smoothest of transitions. It would even help if he would just give me a more obvious heads-up when he was about to nudge me out of the nest. After all, he is the one who created me, and he knows how I like to ease my way into change.

But because he is the God of the unexpected and I am his child who lives by faith, I am learning to lean deeper into the wonder and follow the wind of the Spirit's leading. After all, when God calls me to go, I have found there is nothing worth going back for anyway. It doesn't always make the first steps easier, but it certainly makes the footing more secure.

I have heard many a well-delivered sermon that ended with an invitation for seekers to come forward. The services I recall most vividly involved musicians playing softly while the worship leader sang a carefully chosen song of surrender. Usually somewhere around the second verse, the preacher would come back to the pulpit as the music continued to play and once again address the congregation. He would say things like, "While we tarry . . ." or "If you will reach out to Jesus, he will reach out to you," or maybe even, "We're going to sing that verse one more time and if no one comes, we're going to close." Maybe your pastor even used the line that used to keep me awake at night when I was a kid: "If you got killed in a car wreck on the way home tonight, do you know where you would spend eternity?"

While all of those may be valid statements and questions (even if the approach may have in some cases been suspect), there was one line that especially caught my attention as a young seeker. It went something like, "If you will just take the first step by faith, God will walk the rest of the way with you." It was not only a great visual, but one with precedent.

A hemorrhaging woman pushing her way through a crowd, a tax collector running toward a sycamore tree, a fisherman not afraid to get his feet wet on the Sea of Galilee—what they all had in common was a steadfast refusal to let the last chapter keep them from experiencing the next chapter, even when the next chapter seemed anything but fair.

Cliff was a pastor whose journey to the pulpit was untraditional. Even though he was born and raised in a Bible-believing evangelical family, his teen years were consumed by the deceptive allure of drugs and alcohol. Over time, the fervent prayers of a righteous family and the unrelenting pursuit of a God who loved him would once again affect a heart in need of healing. His "come to Jesus" moment took place at his grandmother's grave in an Ohio cemetery, with no one there but him and the God he had forsaken.

There was nothing halfway about Cliff's prayer or surrender. He wanted all of God and wanted God to have all of him. The transformation was far-reaching. The uncertainty about how or why the Lord could possibly use him did not dim his commitment or the certainty of his call. At the time he could hardly have imagined all the first steps the days ahead would hold. As it turned out, God had been saving a group of teens for him to minister to at a nearby church. Although Cliff would be the first to tell you he did not know specifically what being a youth pastor required, even then, the hand and voice of God were unmistakable.

The days and years ahead would reveal a fascinating flurry of first steps and blessings. He would enroll at an evangelical Bible college where he could study the Word as it continued to impact his daily life. He would fall in love with Karen, who would not only share his name, but also his conviction about taking the gospel to the lost. As God continued to bless the ministry opportunities, he also blessed their home with children. For the first time in a long time, everything finally seemed like it was beginning to make sense.

When the church they were serving announced plans to take a mission trip to the Dominican Republic, no one was surprised that Cliff signed up to go. After all, he had been on several of these trips before, and this one would take him back to the same school he had taken some teenagers to a few years earlier.

There is no way Cliff could have known the extent to which everything in his world was about to change. On that trip, a blood contamination accident left him infected with the dreaded HIV virus.

In the mid-'90s, treatments for HIV were highly experimental and often ineffective. Cliff's fears that the stigma alone would mean the end of his ministry were more than justified. As his condition continued to worsen, he and Karen, along with their children, decided the time had come for one more first step. They moved from Ohio to Florida as they waited for God's healing.

Even though he was too weak for a full-time pastorate, Cliff was still committed to his call to ministry. God was not done with him yet. On the streets of Lakeland, Florida, Cliff and his friend Steve Wade would begin a ministry to the homeless and drug-dependent. The disease that raged within his own body softened his heart for others who were suffering. Cliff Lafferty's healing finally came on January 10, 2002. At the time of this writ-

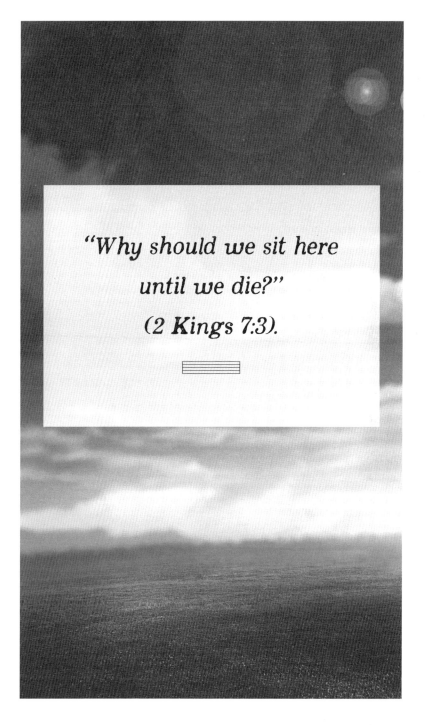

"Why should we sit here
until we die?"
(2 Kings 7:3).

ing, God is still using the Mission-Possible ministry Cliff helped found to tell the story of Jesus to the desolate and unloved.

It is impossible not to think about Cliff when I read 2 Kings 7, which tells the story of four men with leprosy living in exile outside the city gates of Samaria. If you are not familiar with this story, I encourage you to go back and take a look at the preceding passages to get a more accurate picture of what life was like for these four men. Because their disease would have prevented them from entering the city, they formed their own little leper colony outside the city wall, where they lived on scraps of garbage lowered down from the city. And then, as if life were not bad enough for them, the famine of the day reached such extreme proportions even the scraps of food disappeared.

This passage contains a powerful account of Elisha's faith, but also a reminder of the abundant grace of God. My favorite line in the story is found at the point of total desperation. One of the lepers looked at the other and said, "Why should we sit here until we die?" (2 Kings 7:3). Scripture tells us that the leper pressed his case even further by explaining that if they were to go into the city where the famine was, they would die, and if they were to stay where they were, they would also die. On the other hand, if they were to go to the Aramean camp and surrender, they would at least have a chance. We are not told exactly how the other lepers responded, but we do know what they did. These four men, bearing the scars of their infirmities and driven more by determination than promise, lowered the weight of their withered bodies onto their disease-ridden feet and did the only thing they could do: They took the first step. Then they took another step. And then, just when it would have been easy to give up and give in, they took another step. They found that God had already prepared a feast and was just waiting for them to act.

If you listen closely, God is inviting you to take his hand and go for a walk. He wants you to feast at the banquet. At times you may feel like the road is leading you in circles, but don't let go of his hand. When all you can hear is silence, don't stop listening for his voice. Sometimes in this journey of faith, even the most fervent followers need to be reminded that the first step is never the destination—it merely prepares us for the second step.

TEN

Trusting God with "Yes"

So do not fear, for I am with you; do not be dismayed, for I am your God. I will strengthen you and help you; I will uphold you with my righteous right hand (Isaiah 41:10, NIV).

I am a believer. My life can best be described as a one-day-at-a-time process of surrender, of learning what it means to live by saying "yes" to God. This "yes" allows me a front-row seat to watch God work, to hear when he calls, and to follow where he leads. It means listening and responding in obedience. I wish I could say that every "yes" on this journey has been offered with a thunderous hallelujah of unwavering faith; however, I suspect I am not alone in admitting that has not always been the case.

Had I allowed my initial expectations of the Christian life to be defined by the loudest voices, I would have set myself up for some serious disappointments. Maybe their faith was that much stronger than mine. But I am more inclined to believe that the difference was they had learned the secret of "yes." And what exactly is that secret?

For me, discovering the answer began by narrowing all the questions down to one: Do you trust God? Ask most people that question and they will more than likely say yes. When pressed further, the natural inclination is to start specifying what we trust him for, such as food to eat and air to breathe. We trust him for grace when we need it and forgiveness when we ask. The question of what we trust him with can also trigger a checklist of spiritual-sounding bullet points. We claim to trust him with our families and our futures, our dreams and our heartaches. They are all great answers—and yet it is possible for each of these to sidestep the original question: Do you trust God? It's a simple question that requires a not-so-simple response. The "yes" God is longing for requires more than lip service—it requires a complete, heart-first commitment.

For some, it is more palatable to ease into the question. Do you trust that God made the heavens and the earth? That's an easy "yes." Do you trust that he really loves you and wants the best for you? "Yes" without reservation. Do you trust that he is working in all things? Not a problem.

At that point the "yeses" are starting to flow pretty easily, and maybe you are starting to wonder what all the fuss is about. Then life begins to settle in, and if we are not careful, our responses can tend to get tepid or come with selfish conditions. We might not say it out loud, but the unguarded heart begins contemplating things such as how much easier it would be to trust God with our finances if he would only bless us with more money, or how we could trust him with our future if he would just tell us how today is going to work out.

One of the great ironies of the believer's life is how easy it is to trust God with the big-ticket items like the sun rising or the earth rotating on its axis. Yet sometimes it's a whole lot tougher to trust him with things that are up close and personal. When the job that once felt like an answered prayer begins to feel more like a dead end, do you still trust him with it? As you wait for the pathologist's phone call, do you still put your faith in the One who created you? Do you trust him with your children as they back out of the driveway and merge their way into five o'clock rush hour?

While it would be plausible to write an entire chapter on the question "Do you trust God with _____?" (fill in the blank), the secret to living in the "yes" of God's will is taking the qualifiers out of the equation. Do you trust God? No caveats, no conditions, and no compromises.

Scripture is full of variations on this theme. In Genesis 17, God commanded Abraham to "walk before [him] faithfully, and be blameless" (v. 1). Living blamelessly means being completely devoted to one pursuit.

To the psalmist David, walking blamelessly was the standard for the believer's life (Psalm 15:2). Paul prayed that the Philippians would remain pure and blameless until the day of Christ (1:9-11). It was a way of life for Zechariah (Luke 1:6) and a fitting description of Job (1:1).

For those who have yet to acknowledge God's voice, the concept of trusting him with "yes" is a mystery that defies reason. It would be like trying to explain the look of the wind or the sound of silence. The fact that they exist does not make them any easier to explain.

Sometimes Trusting God with "Yes" Means Saying "No"

My friend Bill is a novelist, and a very successful one. He is highly skilled in the art of imagination and, with the simple stroke of a pen, allows each reader to peer through his mind's eye. We first met several years back when we were both booked to teach at a writer's conference. In the years that followed, we found ourselves scheduled at enough of the same events to build a friendship. Even though he wrote mysteries while I preferred rhyme, we had a mutual respect for each other's approach and abilities.

It had been a few years since we had worked together, so I was glad to see Bill sitting in the back row of the auditorium at a Colorado writer's event. Because the keynote speaker was already two points into his speech when I arrived, I took the seat beside Bill and looked forward to catching up after the talk had finished. But that was not at all how the next few minutes played out.

Without so much as a shred of a customary greeting, Bill looked at me and asked a direct question: "So what are you going to do about it?" Even though I wanted to turn around and see if he could have been talking to someone else, I knew the question was aimed squarely at me. "What do you mean?" I asked. Once again he responded with near indignation. "I think you know what I mean. So what are you going to do about it?" I tried to read his demeanor to see if this was a joke, but my instincts told me he was dead serious. The dialogue that followed read like a poorly written interrogation script from a B-movie.

Bill: What are you going to give up?

Me: I'm still not sure what you mean.

Bill: How long has it been since you've slept?

Me: It's been awhile.

Bill: How long do you think you can keep going like this?

Me: I don't know.

Bill: Is the music going well?

Me: Better than I could have dreamed.

Bill: Haven't you always prayed that God would bless the music?

Me: Yes.

Bill: So what are you going to give up?

Me *[insert tears]*: I guess I've never been very good at saying
"no." I'm just not sure which is the one thing that will
lead me to the next thing.

Bill: Don't you think the God you asked to bless your music
and the God that heard and answered those prayers is big
enough to help you know his will for you?

Me *[insert more tears]*: Yes.

Bill: Sometimes God wants you to lie back in the stream and
just let him direct the current. *[Insert big smile.]* Good to
see you, Dave. How have you been?

In a perfect world, these wise words from a trusted friend
would have forever altered the trajectory of my thinking as well as
my work habits. What I have learned, however, is that even though
I can know and say all the right things, this is a place of personal
weakness where Satan knows I have always been susceptible. Over
and over again I am reminded that sometimes trusting God with
"yes" means learning when to say "no" to other things.

If you have served in any level of ministry, whether paid or
volunteer, leader or implementer, you have already learned that
this is not an area where the church offers much assistance. If
you are willing to work, the church's tendency is to let you work
and work and then work some more. If you have a specific gifting
or spiritual strength, that is even better. The only thing we love
more than someone who is willing and gifted is if that person also
happens to be new to the church. Like vultures waiting for some
fresh meat, we love to find those so committed to "yes" they do
not realize "no" is an option. We ask too much of too few far too
early, then act shocked when they burn out or leave the church.
There is a vast difference between the "yes" God requires and
the "yes" others (including the church) ask for.

Trusting God with "yes" ultimately comes down to putting
all our weight on him, including the gifts we have been entrusted

with and the weaknesses we struggle with. He can take it—all our flaws and frailties and our doubts and fears. He is up to the task.

The life of the believer is the life of one who has discovered the sweetness of surrender as God intended. It is not a journey for the weak of heart, but for those courageous enough to risk everything for one word. The word is "yes." Do you trust him?

ELEVEN

In the Waiting

Go from your country and your kindred and your father's house
to the land that I will show you (Genesis 12:1).

When President Richard M. Nixon wrote his memoirs, he chose an interesting opening line. He simply stated, "I was born in the house my father built." Most of our children will never make that claim, yet many will be able to say that they lived in one house from the time of their childhood to adolescence. Nestled in a middle-class neighborhood about thirty miles north of Nashville, the third house on the right is where life has happened for our family for the past twenty years.

Because we live on a dead-end street, or as I prefer to call it, the road to nowhere, the small contingent of neighbors has grown pretty close through the years. The essence of our collective story is captured with phrases like, "We're going to have a baby," or "Amy got her driver's license," or "Cortney's coming to live with us," or "Looks like Cortney's moving out." We have ordered Girl Scout cookies off the same white page, survived runaway puppies, kids going off to college, and practical jokes, and leaned on each other during moments of grief.

One of the more memorable adventures from our side of the street began with a late-night call from our neighbor Jimmy. For more than a decade, he and his wife have lived in the house to the right of ours. Because both our schedules involve a lot of traveling, we have always had a mutual understanding to keep an eye on the other's house when one of us is away. I suspected something must be wrong because it was late when the phone rang and I knew he was out of town at the time. The tone in Cindi's voice as she talked to him only seemed to verify my suspicions. I was already putting my shoes and socks on when I heard Cindi ask if the police were on the way.

The story behind the phone call was fairly simple. Their alarm had gone off and automatically triggered a phone call to Jimmy from the security company, which also automatically called the police department. Although my response seemed like the right thing at the time, in hindsight, what happened next can only be described as comical.

Try and imagine the scene: forsaking any concern for my own safety, I bolted from the front door into the deep of the night, heart racing, leapt across the ditch in a single bound, and raced up the driveway, prepared to take on any criminal that had dared to violate the sanctity of our neighborhood. But as I reached the corner of the house, I was stopped dead in my tracks by a wall of reality.

It suddenly occurred to me that in my urgency to be the protector of all things good and righteous, I was completely and utterly unprepared for any impending encounter. Surely my weapon of choice, a Sears flashlight, would be less than equal to the challenge. Should hand-to-hand combat be required, I was definitely the wrong guy for the job, and besides that, it suddenly dawned on me that there was also a risk of actually getting hurt.

Fortunately, the end of the story is not nearly as dramatic as the beginning. A cat had evidently triggered the alarm and the police showed up in sufficient time for me to retain my man card and some semblance of dignity. I returned home softly singing a line from the old hymn "Leaning on the Everlasting Arms" that says, "Safe and secure from all alarms."

I still can't help but laugh when I think back on that sequence of events. The sad part is that I have seen similar scenarios when it comes to ministry. God calls and we respond. So far so good. But when God's timing doesn't line up with our expectations, things can begin to break down.

"God, you called me to preach. Why haven't you given me a church?"

"Lord, how come just about the time I said yes, you seemed to go silent on me? I am waiting to serve; tell me where."

Maybe you have even wondered whether God really called you to begin with. Everything within us wants to go racing out the door to conquer the darkness with just a flashlight, when perhaps we are not as prepared as we think.

I am convinced that some of the most defining steps in a believer's journey can be found in the waiting—the moments between the anointing and the appointing. Sometimes it is quicker than we expect. Other times we might start to wonder why God would allow his children to walk down a road to nowhere.

It is fascinating to look at everything the psalmist David accomplished in the twenty years from when he was first anointed by Samuel to when he actually became king of Israel. It wasn't like he spent his time pacing around the gates of the temple, wondering what was taking so long. No, he was far too busy for that. He was doing things like taking down giants, running from rulers, living in caves, and renewing covenants.

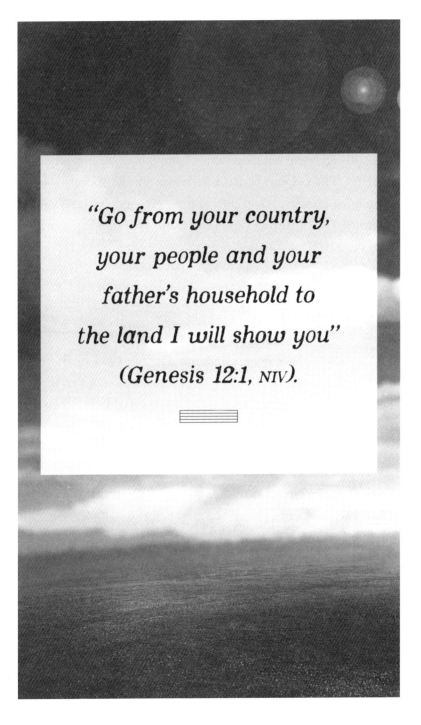

"Go from your country,
your people and your
father's household to
the land I will show you"
(Genesis 12:1, NIV).

I look back at my own life, and except for the whole becoming-a-king business, I see some pretty interesting parallels. When God called me, I was still pretty young. I could have just accepted that call, sat back, and waited for the doors to success to swing wide open. After all, who could have blamed me? God had called me to write. Surely it was going to happen regardless of what I did.

I am so thankful that is not how God works. He invited me into the process, and unlike my daring dash into the neighbor's yard, it did not happen immediately. Not only did God have a specific destination in mind for my call; I am convinced that he is just as concerned about who I am becoming along the way.

While I would not attempt to impress anyone with my limited knowledge of Hebrew, there are a few significant phrases I have picked up through the years. One of these is *lekh lakha* (pronounced *leck lay-HAH*), and it literally translates as "Go forth." It is used two times in Scripture—once at the beginning, and once at the end of the story of Abraham. When God called Abram to leave his home in Ur of the Chaldeans, he said, "Go from your country, your people and your father's household to the land I will show you" (Genesis 12:1, NIV). In Genesis 22:2, the call comes to Abraham again: "Take your son, your only son Isaac, whom you love, and go to the land of Moriah."

In both situations the call was *lekh lakha*, go forth, but what they also had in common was that God did not reveal a specific location. In chapter 12, the command was to go "to the land I will show you," and in chapter 22, it was simply to "go to the land of Moriah." One of the pieces of Abraham's story that is too often overlooked is that when God called him to go to a place God would reveal to him, Abraham got up the next morning and saddled his donkey (Genesis 22:3). He didn't hesitate, lay out a fleece, or attempt to negotiate with God. He didn't even know for sure what the final destination would be. He just went forth.

There is another Hebrew phrase embedded within this story of astonishing sacrifice and exemplary faithfulness. The word is *hinneni* (pronounced *HIN-i-nee*) and it translates simply as "Here I am." One of the themes woven throughout the entire narrative is one of God calling and Abraham responding *hinneni:*

"Abraham, are you willing to leave your family behind?"

"*Hinneni.*"

"Abraham, are you listening?"

"*Hinneni.*"

"Abraham, I want you to take your son, your only son Isaac, and offer him as a sacrifice."

Some read this account and wonder what kind of father could agree to this and, furthermore, what kind of God would even ask this to begin with. Here's the secret: this was not Abraham's first trip up the mountain. By this point, he and God had a well-established, time-tested relationship of trust. I also cannot help but wonder if the level of faith required for such a test was the reason God waited one hundred years to call Abraham to Moriah. Whatever the reason for the testing or the timing, Abraham's answer was the same: "*Hinneni*—Here I am, Lord."

If I had lived my life with the faith of Abraham, I like to think there are some things I would have done a little differently. I might have walked a little more confidently through my valleys when the shadow eclipsed the light. Maybe I would have more quickly forsaken some comfort zones and abandoned some agendas along the way. Maybe instead of rushing out the front door to try and save the world in my own strength, I would have responded with "*Hinneni. . . .* Here I am, Lord. Though in my weakness I wonder, in your strength I am comforted. Waiting. Trusting. Ready to be led to a place you will show me . . . in your timing."

Several years ago, I found myself isolated in what I feared was a one-step-forward, two-steps-back season with God. The allure of my call seemed muted by the uncertainty of waiting. As has always been my nature, I reached for a pencil and some close friends to help write what I could not otherwise say. This was the result:

> *I want a peace beyond my understanding*
> *I want to feel it fall like rain*
> *In the middle of my hurting*
> *I want to feel your arms as they surround me*
> *And let me know that it's okay*
> *To be in here in this place*
> *Resting in the peace that only comes*
> *In the waiting.*[1]
>
> —Clark/Koch/Long

TWELVE

Sometimes the Church Needs You

But we have this treasure in clay jars, so that it may be made clear that this extraordinary power belongs to God and does not come from us (2 Corinthians 4:7).

The legendary Chet Atkins was one of the most influential guitar players in history, and also one of the most quotable. One of my favorite stories about him goes like this: A lady came up one night while he was playing and commented on how beautiful the guitar sounded. He stopped playing, looked her in the eye, and said, "How good does it sound now?" The inference was that it was not the instrument itself, but the player that made it sound beautiful.

When it comes to using our gifts in the service of God's kingdom, this is a powerful and truthful illustration—in reverse. We were created to be instruments of a sovereign God, but when the music (i.e., ministry) is working well, heaven help us if we think it is or ever was about us. This would be an easy place to take potshots at professional pastors and personality-driven pulpits, but I am not convinced that the danger of "look-at-me" ministry is isolated to leadership. It may also reside in the seat beside you or the choir loft. You may even have seen traces of it in the mirror.

The singer delivers a stirring power ballad and the applause from the congregation is spontaneous and unanimous. The preacher presents a homiletic masterpiece as the boisterous sounds of amen waft across the sanctuary. Maybe your youth group is the talk of the high school cafeteria, or maybe your church's food bank for the homeless has been featured on the local news. These are all great things, and I absolutely love to see how God uses such myriad gifts and personalities to edify the church. But I also think we have a responsibility to differentiate between the gift and the Giver. The most effective service we can give will always be that which is offered in humility. I am all about the pursuit of excellence in ministry, but if all we achieve in the process is building each other up, we have missed the mark entirely.

Paul writes in Ephesians 4:12-13 that we should "equip the saints . . . for building up the body of Christ," with the end result being that "all of us come to the unity of the faith and of the knowledge of the Son of God, to maturity, to the measure of the full stature of Christ." In the second chapter of Acts, which describes believers in the early church breaking bread and praying and praising God, we are told that it was the Lord who "added to their number" daily (v. 47).

I acknowledge that most of those reading this already know and believe God to be responsible for whatever good we may accomplish. So why include it in this chapter? The answer is simple. I haven't met many people through the years who feel overqualified for the place of service God has called them to. Most people I have met—and those who this book is primarily geared toward—struggle with the opposite problem. If you are at all like me, you too wrestle with feeling underqualified. We don't struggle with remembering where our gifts come from, but we need to be reminded that God does not leave us to fend for ourselves.

If God calls me to preach, it is my responsibility to study and prepare to be the best preacher I can be, no matter the size of the congregation, then trust God to speak through my words to those who need to hear. If I am playing guitar in the band, I want to use whatever ability I possess to help lead others in worship, even when I feel I'm not as good as the rest of the band. If I am directing cars in the church parking lot, I pray God sees it as an offering of humble service from one of his children. No matter where I am called to serve or what God has gifted me with, I find confidence knowing it is not about me, and that success will not be measured by what I bring to the table.

There is an old adage preachers use to encourage believers: "God does not call the equipped, but instead, he equips the called." I have been so thankful for that truth throughout the years. Back in the eighties I traveled for five years with a musical group called the Speer Family. All these years later, I am still amazed that they were willing to take my mediocre-at-best talent and give me a place to grow in my music as well as my life.

The manager of the group, Brock Speer, had a saying he would periodically pull out if we were getting a little rambunctious. He would say, "Don't ever forget that you need the church more than the church needs you." It was his not-so-subtle way of reminding us that the church could have called any one of a hundred different guests to come, but they had invited us. It was a privilege to be there, and we needed to act accordingly. I always thought that was a pretty solid perspective and a natural fit for someone like me.

Because everything about my life seemed built around the church, including my closest friendships and the fact that my love for music was nurtured on its platform, this was an easy philosophy to adopt. It was through the church I would eventually meet Cindi, and as far as our kids can reach in either direction of their family tree, they will find the church. I would be the first to agree that yes, I need the church more than the church needs me.

After leaving the Speers, I spent many years traveling by myself on weekends ministering in churches, ever mindful of just how blessed I was to be there. Even during those years, I knew that if a church was allowing me to come and share, it was not about any exceptional talent I had to offer. In fact, knowing that it wasn't about me made it easier to celebrate what God was doing through the ministry.

Things were going along pretty well until a phone call came in the fall of 2002. It was a pastor I did not know calling from a church I did not attend. He told me that God had laid my name on his heart to lead worship at his church. He said he was new in town and there wasn't much money for music or salary, but he wondered if I was willing to meet with him and talk about it. Within minutes of sitting down at a nearby restaurant, we both felt a peace that God was in the middle of it all.

Although I was certain God had ordained the roads leading up to that moment, I also had to come to terms with something I had not expected. Based on everything he was saying, it seemed like the church needed me. This was an idea I had never encountered before. Here was the problem: Up until that time, in life and in ministry, it had been pretty easy to accept that I needed the church. It was a whole lot tougher thinking that the church needed me.

In the years since I first stepped onto that church platform, I have continued to learn what it means to live in the expectancy of God. I cannot be content as a mere bystander when God has called me to be a participant. I do not have to know where he is leading; I just have to trust that he is. I don't have to be the best singer in the choir or give the most money in the offering, volunteer the most hours at church, or say "amen" the loudest on Sunday morning. What God wants most is for me to take the gifts he has blessed me with and use them to the best of my ability to edify the body of Christ. . . . and then stand back and watch God do what God does from the best seat in the house.

When my son Sam was still pretty small, I bought him one of those big, red, plastic baseball bats. It was light enough that he could swing it but big enough to hit the ball fairly easily. On one particular evening as we engaged in a routine of living room home-run derby, Sam seemed to have trouble putting the bat on the ball. I would pitch and he would swing. Whiff! I pitched again and he missed it again. After several successive misses I could see the frustration building and knew I needed to come up with something. I took one more look at that bat and it dawned on me that if he would just hold the bat still, I felt pretty certain I could hit it. I said, "Sam, this time I want you to hold the bat but don't swing." He grabbed the handle of that big old bat and held it up like the whole world was watching. I reared back and the ball went straight from my hand to the head of that bat. BAM! The plastic baseball bounced off the bat like a laser sailing deep into the recesses of the upper deck (translation: over the white recliner by the window). He threw the bat across the living room floor and ran the base paths as if he had just won the World Series.

Through the years I have seen enough attitude and ego from those serving in ministry to last me the rest of my life. Where I serve is not "my" church or "my" ministry. I am simply a caretaker entrusted with a precious commodity. When we work to the best of our ability to use the gifts God has given us, it's like he is letting us hold the bat. Even though he is the one doing all the work, he graciously allows us to throw the bat, run the bases, and scream and holler as if we won the game and did it all on our own.

In 2 Corinthians 4:7, we are reminded that "we have this treasure in clay jars, so that it may be made clear that this extraordinary power belongs to God and does not come from us."

Put me in, Coach. . . . I think I'm ready.

THIRTEEN

How Big Is God?

The Lord your God is with you, the Mighty Warrior who saves.
He will take great delight in you; in his love he will no longer
rebuke you, but will rejoice over you with singing
(Zephaniah 3:17, NIV).

The faithful Wednesday night crowd had gathered in the fire-side room of the small Midwestern church. After everyone sang a few hymns together, the pastor looked around the room and asked if there were any prayer requests. It was his wife who spoke up first. While it was not uncommon for her to share a particular burden she was carrying, as she began to speak, it was evident that something was different about this night. Everyone in the room knew that their youngest daughter was born deaf, but even so, she began by sharing the story once again. She said she had always believed that one day God would heal their daughter, even though it had not happened yet. But healing was not her request that evening.

Through tears, she began to share about what at the time was a new technological device called a TTY—a portable modem with a small keyboard and LED display that allowed the hearing impaired to use the telephone. Her dilemma was a simple matter of faith. If they were to purchase a device that was sure to make their daughter's life easier, would it mean they lacked faith that God could heal her?

It has now been thirty years since I sat as a curious onlooker in that Wednesday night prayer meeting. Even though the technology she was wrestling with now seems antiquated, the story grips me still. Why? Because I think her vulnerability encapsulated an all-too-real quandary for believers. After all, if the pastor's wife—a courageous stalwart of the faith—was capable of exposing such a visible weakness, could the rest of us really be safe?

One of the realities I had to come to grips with years ago is that none of us are quite as strong as we like to think. Even Christ-followers can fall into the trap of claiming to give everything over to God, only to find themselves continuing to suffocate from hurt, worry, and struggle over things that hurt, worry, and struggle have no discernible effect on. Like you, I have watched the mere mention of the word "cancer" reduce even the mightiest among us to emotional rubble. The same evening news that once brought us information now seems intent on bringing the fears of the world into our living room in real time. Things we were told were healthy only yesterday top today's warning list, and we wonder how we can be at fault for doing what naturally humans do—fear!

If you are like me, when worry is at its peak, it seems like without fail, someone with the best of intentions will remind you of 1 Peter 5:7: "Cast all your anxiety on him because he cares for you" (NIV). The perceived insinuation is that you are obviously not as spiritual as he or she is or you would already be in casting mode. The truth is that even we as believers need to be reminded that God really is concerned about what we are going through. One of the perks of being a child of God is that by virtue of our relationship with him, we are entitled to cast all of our burdens on him. That does not mean we cherry-pick which of our struggles we relinquish to God any more than God chooses which ones he is willing to accept. But when we reach the point of trusting God enough to lay everything at his feet, some pretty amazing things begin to happen.

God Will Sustain Us

One of the more consoling passages in Scripture is found in Psalm 55:22: "Cast your cares on the Lord and he will sustain you; he will never let the righteous be shaken" (NIV). Other translations use phrases such as "he will take care of you" (NCV) or "he will support you (CEB)," but the inference is the same. The one who knows us best loves us most and will walk beside us through our darkest storms. Allison, our oldest child, was just a few months old when, like all other new parents, we took her in for the shots that evidently are required. As would become our routine in the years ahead, I drove Cindi and Allison to the doctor and waited patiently for them in the car until they were finished. My reasoning for remaining outside, although I am not necessarily proud of it, was pretty simple: I knew there was no way I could stand by and watch someone put a needle into my baby's arm. In fact, I could not even sit in the waiting room just in case I were to hear her scream.

As usual, Cindi's response was completely the opposite. She believed if the shot was going to keep Allison healthy, the long-term gain was worth the momentary pain. She also insisted that if Allison had to have a shot, she wanted to hold her through it so that Allison would know that she was there for her and that she was not going through it alone.

Even though the anecdote accurately portrays me as the weak-kneed father that I am, it also serves as a great illustration of the love of God in our lives. Even in our weakest moments, he does not forsake us but chooses instead to hold us through our pain.

God Will Protect Us

To the casual historian, Martin Luther's legacy is too often reduced to the ninety-five theses he attached to a church door in Wittenberg, Germany, accusing the Catholic church of heresy. But his impact goes much deeper than that one event. His personal impact on the Protestant movement as we know it is immeasurable. Yet for all of his positive influence, in his early years he wrestled with a deep fear of the wrath of God. As one who at that point had not experienced faith, he came to resent the very idea of it.

Out of his personal turmoil, the man known as the great reformer would write the lyrics for one of my favorite hymns, "A Mighty Fortress Is Our God." Sometimes, in our desire to reduce the old songs to the lowest level of accessibility, we sacrifice the penetrating imagery of the original lyrics. On the other hand, sometimes our failure to fully understand the original lyrics keeps us from experiencing the full impact of the hymn.

Luther's original lyric, referred to by some as the "Battle Hymn of the Reformation," was written in German and translated into English by Frederic H. Hodge 250 years later. The theme of the song is Satan's unrelenting pursuit for the soul of man, as seen in the well-known opening stanza:

A mighty Fortress is our God,

A Bulwark never failing;

Our helper He, amid the flood

Of mortal ills prevailing.

For still our ancient foe

Doth seek to work us woe;

His craft and power are great,

And, armed with cruel hate,

On earth is not his equal.

Martin Luther was not the first to recognize this ongoing battle between light and darkness but found hope and the inspiration in the words of Psalm 46:

God is our refuge and strength, a very present help in trouble. Therefore we will not fear, though the earth should change, though the mountains shake in the heart of the sea; though its waters roar and foam, though the mountains tremble with its tumult. There is a river whose streams make glad the city of God, the holy habitation of the Most High. God is in the midst of the city; it shall not be moved; God will help it when the morning dawns. The nations are in an uproar, the kingdoms totter; he utters his voice, the earth melts. The Lord of hosts is with us; the God of Jacob is our refuge. (Vv. 1-7)

In the most troublesome days of the Reformation, Luther would find great consolation in the same promise that is available to us today: The God who sustains us will also protect us against the storm that rages.

God Will Restore Us

One of my most treasured possessions is a Martin D28 guitar. Admittedly, that brand or body style may not mean much to a nonmusician, but to anyone who has ever played, the name alone summons a healthy level of appreciation. Besides the name on the headstock, there is another even more significant reason why it holds such value for me.

This particular guitar was a gift from a friend of our family when I was in tenth grade. Walt was an alcoholic who worked at the same factory as my father, yet after a life-altering encounter with a transforming God, he put down the bottle forever. After years of drinking away any excess income (in his words), he decided it was time to put his money to a better use. I vividly recall the day he called me to his house and told me I was going to need a

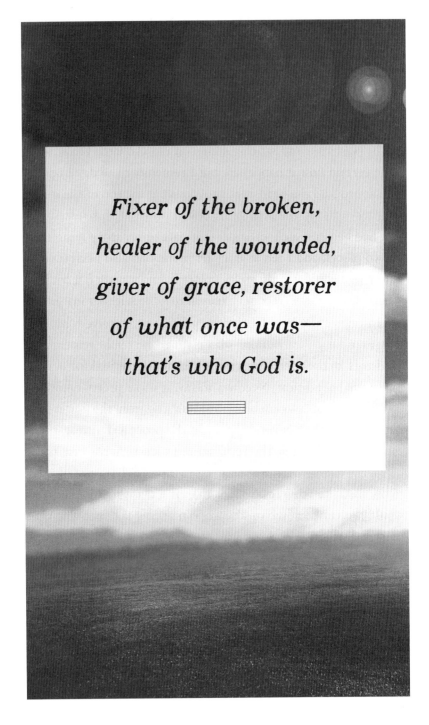

Fixer of the broken, healer of the wounded, giver of grace, restorer of what once was— that's who God is.

better guitar if I was going to move to Nashville and write songs. He knew I was a fan of Johnny Cash, and because Johnny Cash played a Martin D28, Walt decided that is what I should have as well. As any good musician knows, a guitar of any significance should have a name, and Goliath was the name I chose for mine.

It was only a few years later that I found myself actually living in Nashville and writing songs on old Goliath. I'm still not quite certain how it happened, but I remember the day I opened the case to find the headstock broken off at the top of the guitar, attached only by the strings. I looked down at this instrument that had become such an important part of my story lying there in two pieces, and I felt as if a part of me had also been severed. Knowing I could not afford to replace it, and unsure *if* it could be repaired, I began to reconcile myself to a life without my guitar.

In one of the best Christmas gifts I ever received, my parents found a guitar builder who claimed he could reattach the headstock to the neck and bring it back to its original form, if not its original condition. Needless to say, it was a pretty emotional Christmas to once again hear music coming from the guitar I had feared was broken beyond repair. In the process, I also learned a valuable lesson about the restoration process. According to the builder, the glue used to bond the two pieces back together actually made the guitar stronger than it was originally, but there would forever be a line on the wood marking the spot where the damage had been done.

Fixer of the broken, healer of the wounded, giver of grace, restorer of what once was—that's who God is. Like the guitar builder, he longs to take the pieces of our past that were broken and useless and not only restore them into something of value, but make them even stronger than they were originally. Yes, sometimes there are scars that remain, but they serve as fitting reminders of just how far God has brought us from who we used to be. I love the words in 1 Peter 5:10 that remind us, "And after you have suffered for a little while, the God of all grace, who has called you to his eternal glory in Christ, will himself restore, support, strengthen, and establish you."

So, I wonder, which God is yours? Is he the one you allow to come into the doctor's office with you? Or do you make him wait outside? Are you intimidated by a God who knows you so well? Or are you comforted that he knows you that well, yet still loves you? Are you content to be defined by the brokenness of your past? Or are you finally ready to be restored? Are you satisfied with a God who is simply able to meet your need, or are you ready to experience someone who "is able to do *exceedingly* abundantly above all that *we* ask or think" (Ephesians 3:20, NKJV, emphasis added)? No matter how big you dream God is, he is bigger. No matter how much forgiveness your past requires, it is already covered. And just when you think he cannot love you any more than he already does, he will.

One of the lesser-known lyrics from the great hymn writer Isaac Watts comes from the third verse of "I Sing the Mighty Power of God." I think it says it well:

> *There's not a plant or flower below,*
> *but makes Thy glories known,*
> *And clouds arise, and tempests blow,*
> *by order from Thy throne;*
> *While all that borrows life from Thee*
> *is ever in Thy care;*
> *And everywhere that we can be,*
> *Thou, God, art present there.*

FOURTEEN

A Theology of Weakness

Where is the one who is wise? Where is the scribe? Where is the debater of this age? Has not God made foolish the wisdom of the world? For since, in the wisdom of God, the world did not know God through wisdom, God decided, through the foolishness of our proclamation, to save those who believe (1 Corinthians 1:20-21).

To anyone who doubts that God has a sense of humor, I would point out that for more than three decades I have been married not only to a teacher, but a math teacher. Those who knew me well in my younger days could attest to my long-running feud with x's and y's and all they supposedly represented. There are still days I am convinced that were it not for my sister Sharon, who was a grade ahead of me in school, I would have never made it out of the tenth grade.

It's been a couple of years now since Cindi called me to her classroom to install some new software on her computer. From her desk at the back of the room, I watched and listened as she passionately explained to a room full of seventh graders that x really does equal y (as if they were ever going to need to know this).

I'm old enough to remember the initial rollout of what was known as modern math. What struck me most even then was that it seemed like they were taking something I could understand and complicating it to the point where it became incomprehensible. I couldn't help but think about that as I sat and listened from the back of the room that morning. I am not ashamed to tell you that as I listened, everything in me wanted to stand up and say to these students, "Hey, kids! In all these years, I've never needed to know how to do this." I didn't, however, because I knew it would have meant the end to life as I knew it.

Now that I have offended all the math teachers who might have picked up this book, I will concede that it's probably not that the information is useless. But I wonder what good it does to teach them that x equals y when they can't make change for a five-dollar bill at McDonald's. Here's the problem: When I was younger, I spent all my time learning the concepts, yet no one ever taught me how to apply them. That might help explain why, all these years later, I find myself sitting stoically as Cindi and the kids discuss things like the Pythagorean theorem at the dinner table. Unfortunately, math is not the only area of my life where I've encountered concepts that were once simple yet now seem complicated.

As a frequent clinician at various songwriting conferences and seminars around the country, one of the habits I see in many young songwriters is the taking of simple ideas such as a blue sky and explaining it with big songwriter-sounding words. For me, the great songs are the ones that do the complete opposite. I love it when a writer takes a deep truth of Scripture and writes about it in words that even I can understand. I am much less likely to be impressed by how many big words you know than I am by how much you can say with words I already know. In fact, I have always maintained that one of the best things I have going for me as a songwriter is that I have never been smart enough to write over anyone's head.

If I find this to be true in math and music, could it also spill over into other areas of life—like what it means to be a follower of Christ? Come to church every time the doors are open, sing as loudly as you can during the worship set, and raise both hands in the air just like they do in all those worship slides, and you should be in good shape when you're standing in line at the pearly gates. Okay, I've never heard any of those things actually said in a church, but I fear that is the standard we have adopted for determining who is and who is not a card-carrying member of the brotherhood of believers. The problem is, we are the ones who have added all these things to what Christ intended to be simple.

When one of the scribes asked Jesus which of the commandments was the greatest, Jesus simply responded, "Love the Lord your God with all your heart and with all your soul and with all your mind and with all your strength" (Mark 12:30, niv). In fact, I can't find anywhere in Scripture where Jesus told anyone to go to church on Sunday night or use the hymnal when they sang in order to get to heaven.

If we are not careful, we can so add many things to our "how to be holy" list that we risk losing the joy of the experience and allowing the dialogue to become hijacked by all the wrong questions. I hear some worry about whether you can smoke and be a Christian. Here's the answer: "Love the Lord your God with all your heart and with all your soul and with all your mind and with all your strength." Is it wrong to drink alcohol? "Love the Lord your God with all your heart and with all your soul and with all your mind and with all your strength." Does God expect us to give more than 10 percent? "Love the Lord your God with all your heart and . . ."

When I begin to strip away all the things we have added to the concept of the Christian walk, I find that the application is something even I can get my hands around. It's not a list of dos and don'ts or x equals y—just sheep willing to follow the Shepherd.

According to French politician Georges Bidault, "The weak have one weapon: the errors of those who think they are strong." And according to the apostle Paul in 1 Corinthians 1, "God chose what is foolish in the world to shame the wise; God chose what is weak in the world to shame the strong; God chose what is low and despised in the world, things that are not, to reduce to nothing things that are, so that no one might boast in the presence of God" (vv. 27-29). In other words, the fact that someone else may be smarter, more gifted, or more eloquent doesn't give them any greater access to God's power. He has made it available to people like you and me so that we can claim it and apply in our day-to-day living.

When God calls us, he calls us to a kingdom that at first glance appears completely upside-down from everything we have ever known. If you want to be a leader, become a servant. If you want to live, you must die. If you want to be strong, you must become weak. Somewhere along the way comes the realization that it is actually *our* kingdom that is upside-down; God's has been right-side up all along.

When I was in college, as if I did not already have enough books to read, I found a book called *The Homiletical Plot* by a man named Eugene Lowry. The focus was on developing a narrative style of preaching. One of the illustrations from the book that stuck with me involved a brick wall. The author said that when most people look at a wall, they can tell you the color of the brick and the length and height of the wall, but seldom notice the mortar that holds the brick together.

You have seen it and so have I. Even in ministry, there are times we can become so intent on building a wall to showcase our gifts and abilities that we lose sight of the mortar responsible for all that we have to begin with. We can have the right motivation and end up with the wrong message. We can get so caught up in the concept that we lose the application. We can get so caught up in x equals y that we forget 3 plus 3 equals 6.

I like Paul. I love the way he writes a letter. I can relate to his vulnerability. But I think what I love most of all is how God continues to speak to me at my point of need through the apostle's words. I go back again to 1 Corinthians 1:25-29 and find exactly what I need just when I need it:

> For the foolishness of God is wiser than human wisdom, and the weakness of God is stronger than human strength. Brothers and sisters, think of what you were when you were called. Not many of you were wise by human standards; not many were influential; not many were of noble birth. But God chose the foolish things of the world to shame the wise; God chose the weak things of the world to shame the strong. God chose the lowly things of this world and the despised things—and the things that are not—to nullify the things that are, so that no one may boast before him. (NIV)

These are much-needed words of wisdom written in a way even I can understand, and I suspect I am not alone. One of my favorite verses of Charlotte Elliott's great hymn "Just As I Am" says:

> *Just as I am, tho' tossed about*
> *With many a conflict, many a doubt,*
> *Fightings and fears within, without,*
> *O Lamb of God, I come! I come!*

And so we come—with all our questions. And in him we find understanding. It was never intended to be complicated. It's not a list is dos and don'ts or x equals y—just sheep willing to follow the Shepherd.

FIFTEEN

Jesus Is All I Need

I solemnly urge you: proclaim the message; be persistent whether the time is favorable or unfavorable; convince, rebuke, and encourage, with the utmost patience in teaching (2 Timothy 4:1b-2).

When we are young, we expect to go to funerals of those who are much older than us. Those who are blessed to live to an old age often find themselves attending memorials for those who are younger. I have always maintained that the toughest services to attend are those of friends my age. It's an up-close, way-too-personal reminder just how brief our season on earth is and how quickly it can come to an end.

But that is only part of the reason why this particular Friday afternoon in early May was such a tough one. Jim was my friend. He may have been a few years older, but you would not have guessed it by the way we interacted with each other. We served together on various committees and shared a love for old hymns. He could beat me (or anyone else he played) at golf and would do so with a smile. It was impossible to be around him for any time at all and not feel encouraged—and yet none of us knew the struggle that raged beneath his upbeat demeanor.

Although I arrived early, I found the sanctuary already nearly full, and the organ music coming from the platform seemed to provide a safe cover for the silence in the pews. As I waited for the service to start, I noticed a familiar figure coming toward me.

Dr. Millard Reed was well advanced in years by this point, and I was struck by how time had reduced this once-gregarious pastor and university president to a man who shuffled as he walked, like old men tend to do. I was certain he could not have seen me standing by the door since he had barely lifted his head as he walked, so I was caught off guard when he stopped where I was standing. The words he spoke could hardly have pierced deeper into my already fragile emotions.

"Dave, now is the time for the poets among us to go and write and make sense of all this." Stunned and speechless, I simply nodded my head as he lowered his and continued into the sanctuary. Part of me wanted to call out after him, "Don't put that on my shoulders." Part of me wanted to run to my car where I could cry without being seen. The only thing I was completely sure of was that I did not want to write. What concerned me most was not that I thought he was saying it was up to me to figure out, but that even he, one of the most articulate thinkers I had ever met, was also at a loss for answers.

I thought back to my early days as a young songwriter when my friend Harlan Moore reminded me that, like it or not, a majority of people get their theology from the music they listen to. In both situations, I found myself asking God what have become all-too-familiar questions: Why me? What if I get it wrong? If answers rest even partially on my insight or wisdom, I fear there will be many left stranded by the road.

As a freshman in Bible college, I invested what was for me a sizable amount of money in the latest, greatest collection of digital commentaries. I couldn't wait to share the news with my professor to show him just how committed I was about getting it right. Imagine my frustration when he responded that I should never rely on commentaries, but instead focus on word studies to understand the Word. With that in mind, my next purchase was a home study course in biblical Greek because, after all, if my friend was even a little bit right that someone might be depending on me for theology, the pressure was on. I read and reread Paul's second letter to Timothy, in which he encouraged him, "Do your best to present yourself to God as one approved by him, a worker who has no need to be ashamed, rightly explaining the word of truth" (2 Timothy 2:15). In chapter 4, verse 2 of the same letter, Paul told Timothy (translation mine) to "preach, whether the time feels right or not."

But it didn't end there. I bought an interlinear New Testament, collected books on Hebrew poetry, and even downloaded sermons from preachers with British accents (because we all know the cool accent makes them sound smarter). But I felt no relief.

I'm not sure how many of you have a Bob Broadbooks in your life, but I am thankful I do. Not only is he an influential pastor and a close friend, but we also share a love for great stories. No matter what is on the agenda when we get together, it normally takes a backseat to whatever great story one of us has just heard or experienced. More importantly, he is on a fairly short list of people who always seem to know just what I need to hear at a given moment.

One of those defining conversations took place years ago. I had just finished my first class in Old Testament, and Bob asked how I felt about it. I confessed that the class had left me with a bit of a dilemma and then attempted to explain. I said, "You know I got saved when I was pretty young. Even though I didn't get to go to college when most people do, I have always read and studied the Bible. I have no doubt God called me to write, and I have been doing that to the best of my ability all these years. I have watched God bless it. One Old Testament class gave me just a glimpse of how much I don't know, and now, for the first time in my life, I am afraid to write." I told him that was a pretty scary feeling for me.

In typical Bob fashion, he looked at me without any hesitation and said, "David, now don't take this wrong, but do you really believe for one minute that all these years you were the one writing those songs?" He was absolutely right. All those years, even though I had been claiming to give God the credit for any inspiration or good results, it turned out there was still something in me that believed it came down to my wisdom and ability.

What, then, is the answer? How can I be expected to rightly divide the Word of God when the journey of discovering Scripture is a lifelong pursuit with no end point? For me, the question becomes even more complicated when I hear scholars and theologians—some of whom even share the same denominational beliefs—fundamentally disagree on the interpretation of certain passages of Scripture.

To be honest, I am not sure I know the most theologically correct response to the question. What I do believe, however, is that when the Lord says go, I'd better start moving. Whether I am writing, teaching, or preaching, it is my responsibility to follow the leading of the Holy Spirit even as I continue to "study to shew [myself] approved" to the Lord (2 Timothy 2:15, KJV).

I heard a story of a very successful songwriter who used to write many songs in three-four time signature. When someone asked him why he no longer wrote in three-four after enjoying so much success with that formula, he responded that even though he had gotten away with that for many years, he now knew better.

I can look back at sermons I preached or writing I did that, even though it was at the highest level of my understanding and ability then, is insufficient for what I understand now. When I look back at those efforts and see how God used them, I am reminded again of the old song my father loves to sing, "Little Is Much When God Is in It." God can take and use whatever we give him. It is up to us to give him our very best.

Last summer I spoke at a conference in Atlanta. It had all the makings of an "if something can go wrong it probably will" event. Because of a previous commitment in Nashville, I did not end up leaving town until nearly midnight the night before. Add to that a four-hour drive, losing an hour due to the time change, and an early morning time slot on the program—I knew it was going to be tough couple of days. As it turned out, that would be a significant understatement.

It was about two o'clock in the morning when I noticed the temperature gauge on the rental car beginning to approach the red line. There was very little I could do about it at that time of the night, so I turned off the air conditioning, rolled down the windows, and prayed for God to just get me to Atlanta. I arrived in time for a two-hour nap at the hotel, spoke at the conference, shared lunch with the great folks who had invited me, and made my way to the car to head back to Nashville.

While Friday afternoon traffic in Atlanta carries its own challenges, add to it a severe rainstorm, a car overheating, a driver with two hours' sleep, and you have the potential for a minister of the gospel to lose his salvation. To make matters worse, the computer in the rental car automatically shut off the fans, which allowed the windows to cloud up with no way to defrost them.

Unsure of what to do next, I stuck my head into the downpour so I could see, put my hazard lights on, and continued to drive on the shoulder until the next exit. I found a grocery

*God can take and
use whatever we give him.
It is up to us to give
him our very best.*

store parking lot and called the rental company to come get their broken down, four-door excuse for a car. I was told the only thing they could do was send a wrecker who would then have to take me and this fine piece of machinery all the way back to Atlanta, then another thirty miles south to the airport for a replacement car. By then, I confess, the joy of the Lord was barely a remnant in my attitude.

It was close to an hour before I saw the big red tow truck circle the parking lot. As the driver hooked the chains to the car, I took my place in the cab of the truck and prepared my mind for the next chapter in the odyssey. We were hardly out of the parking lot when I noticed a well-worn King James Version of the Bible on the dash of the truck. Knowing my new friend, Gary, and I were about to spend the next hour together, I asked him what his story was.

"Well, I spent a lot of time in prison for shooting a man and beating up a cop," he began. Needless to say, whatever weariness I was feeling at that point completely vanished. He had my complete attention. Over the next forty-five minutes I listened intently to a story of a mother's persistent prayers and a God who forgives and restores. He told me how God had taken the shambles of a life that could have easily been written off and given him a godly wife, a good job, and, as he called it, his church on wheels. He told me how every morning he walks around that red tow truck and prays that God will put people in his path who need to hear the gospel. He then looked at me and said, "You know, I figure if people are stuck riding with me, I might as well take advantage of the time to witness to them."

He never did ask what I did or where I was headed, and in what seemed like no time at all, we were pulling into the airport. Before I got out he asked if he could pray for me. I told him I would be honored but wondered if he would let me pray for him as well.

There is a pretty good chance I will never cross paths with Gary again on this earth, but he has crossed my mind many times since. He never had the advantage of a college education or a class in systematic theology. He probably won't ever sit in a fancy wingback chair on the church platform or impress the Sunday saints with his grasp of homiletics, but I don't think that matters as much to God as it might to us. What I saw was a minister of the gospel preaching the transforming power of Christ at the level of his experience, day in and day out, from the inside of a red sanctuary at seventy miles an hour.

Too tired to drive home, I got a hotel room where I could process what God was trying to teach me. I had come to minister but instead had been ministered to. I had come to teach, but instead had learned much. I had come to make a difference, but instead I was changed.

> *I'd rather have Jesus than men's applause;*
> *I'd rather be faithful to His dear cause;*
> *I'd rather have Jesus than worldwide fame.*
> *I'd rather be true to His holy name.*
>
> *Than to be the king of a vast domain*
>   *Or be held in sin's dread sway.*
> *I'd rather have Jesus than anything*
>   *This world affords today.*[1]
>
> —Rhea Miller

SIXTEEN

This Is God

*Therefore, there is now no condemnation for those who are
in Christ Jesus, because through Christ Jesus the law of the
Spirit who gives life has set you free from the law of sin
and death* (Romans 8:1-2, NIV).

*It is for freedom that Christ has set us free. Stand firm, then,
and do not let yourselves be burdened again by a yoke of slavery*
(Galatians 5:1, NIV).

If you were to come and visit my church on any given Sunday,
you would find Jason and Kelly in the center section, third row
from the front. They moved to town about five years ago and
first heard about our church from some strangers at a restaurant
(which, by the way, is the original form of social media).

If you lined up Jason's story next to mine, you would think we
had very little in common. After all, he grew up in the sunshine
state of Florida with an alcoholic father who introduced him to
the bottle early in life, while I grew up in Michigan with a father
and mother who introduced me to the Bible early in life. His
conversion story began when he was already grown while mine
started as an eight-year-old boy. His testimony is of what God
delivered him from, and mine includes a whole list of things I

believe God kept me out of through the years. And yet, in spite of our differing journeys, there we stand with equal access to the throne, worshipping the same redemptive God.

Sunday morning in a different church setting, about five hundred miles north of Nashville, you might encounter another friend. Sandi's story is different from both Jason's and mine. She grew up in a strong Bible-believing family where church attendance was a mandatory part of the weekly routine. Any outsider looking in would have thought that all was well, but the facade was soon to be shattered. The unexpected announcement of her parents' divorce could easily have served as the catalyst for Sandi's own downward spiral, but unfortunately, there is more to the story—much more.

It is no secret the scars of molestation go deeper than the surface and that the impact lasts well beyond the act itself, even when the symptoms largely go unnoticed. This was particularly true in Sandi's case. Blessed with an engaging smile and outgoing personality, she was able to maintain the protective fortress around the secret she had been hiding since age four.

She was pregnant at fifteen, a mother at sixteen, had three abortions, and was a battered wife at eighteen. Her feelings of unworthiness only intensified as the chains of abuse continued their grip on her. Another pregnancy would follow, a divorce, a new marriage, an addiction to prescription pills, and then another divorce. If there was a light at the end of the tunnel, Sandi certainly could not see it from where she stood. But something deep within her knew it was still there.

Those who stand beside her this Sunday morning would never imagine the agony Sandi experienced on her way back home. The reason she can lift the songs of praise with such freedom is not because of what she took to the cross, but because of what she left there.

If I could add one more image to this mosaic, it would be Hannah's story. While Sundays also find her in church, she is not seated out front like Jason or Sandi. Hannah is usually the one on the platform leading worship. In fact, while traveling with her family, she has the opportunity to minister to about seventy-five thousand people a year and encourage them in their walk with the Lord. Because Hannah is blessed with extraordinary talent and exceptional beauty, it would be easy to assume the pages of her story based solely on the cover of the book.

While her struggle was not the traditional variety of drugs and alcohol that many teenagers deal with, it held the same devastating potential for ruin. Finding yourself nearly one hundred pounds overweight is never good, but it was particularly troubling for the young, introverted girl with a love for God and a heart for ministry. Even the ceaseless encouragement of a loving father and mother could not seem to break through the wall of self-doubt.

Embedded in the lyrics of one of the songs her family sings is the idea that sometimes it takes a storm to realize your need for shelter. The storm in Hannah's life was one of image and self-esteem, but she found shelter in the reminder that her heavenly Father had fearfully and wonderfully created her. Now she challenges others to rise above complacency when it comes to the unique gifts God has given them and not let the enemy defeat them. After all, it is a lesson she has learned firsthand.

At first glance there appear to be very few similarities in the stories of Jason, Sandi, and Hannah. They are unique individuals shaped by distinct journeys and circumstances, yet here they stand, side-by-side beneath the all-encompassing canopy of God's love. But then, that's always been the nature of grace.

Just look at the twelve disciples. Their group included a corrupt tax collector, a skeptic, a zealot, and a couple of simple fishermen. Peter, one of Jesus' closest companions, would end up denying the one he loved, and Judas would sell his soul for some pieces of silver.

One of the interesting things is just how little we really know about many of them before their encounter with the Master. What we do know is that for the most part, they were just average people who came from varied backgrounds and brought unique gifts, yet answered a single call to follow.

If you were asked to put a name and a story to your definition of grace, I wonder what it would look like and whose name would be attached to it. There are plenty of examples in Scripture, such as Noah receiving God's favor in Genesis 6, or the surprise Esau had for Jacob in Genesis 33. Maybe the first picture that comes to mind is of Jesus drawing in the sand when presented with the adulterous woman. He was not condoning the sin, neither was he condemning the sinner. One by one, as the Pharisees walked away, I can only imagine what they must have been thinking. They had come to cast stones but had witnessed grace instead. These are all good examples—but I wonder, when was the last time you experienced grace with skin on it?

If you were to ask a man named Mehmet Ali Agca what grace looks like, I think I know what his answer would be. His name may not be familiar, but chances are you have heard his story. The day was May 13, 1981, and Pope John Paul II was riding across St. Peter's Square in an open automobile. As the crowd waited to catch a glimpse of him, the buzz of excitement changed to horror as gunshots began to ring out. Hit by four of the bullets and losing a considerable amount of blood, the pope was rushed to a nearby hospital. If there was any good news, it was that before the shooter, Ali Agca, could flee from the crime scene, grace was already at work.

It was later revealed that as even he lay in the ambulance on the way to the hospital, Pope John Paul II forgave a man he did not know for a crime few could have imagined. Four days later, grace was once again in full view as his forgiveness was pronounced in a public setting.

The pope's gesture should have been considered a sufficient example of compassion, but grace, by its very nature, goes above and beyond human expectations. On December 27, 1983, television screens around the world captured the unforgettable picture of Pope John Paul II alone with the accused in a Roman prison cell, offering forgiveness.

To the pundits of the world, that act of forgiveness defied comprehension. They referred to it as selfless and unimaginable, forgiveness of historic proportions. But I understood—I had seen it before. You see, I too was guilty, condemned, and without hope when the only one who could forgive me came all the way to where I was to say it in person. It was a gift from the Father at the cost of his only Son. The only word that can describe it is grace.

Grace is redemptive and forgiving. It is compassionate and long-suffering. It finds us where we are and leads us to places we could never have gone. But that is only the beginning. From diverse journeys we are offered diverse opportunities. From grace received we are called to extend grace.

My mind returns again to the stories of Jason, Sandi, and Hannah, and I am thankful for a God who is much more interested in unity than uniformity. I am glad that he will judge our time on earth not by how we start the race, but by how we finish. I am also thankful for a God who does not differentiate between big sins and small ones or give up on us when we give up on ourselves. We have all been purchased by the same blood, and God sees us only as new creations in him. As if that were not enough, we also have the assurance that he does not leave us where he redeems us, but is continually transforming us into his own image with ever-increasing glory.

What does it mean to live in the image of God? What Jason could not do is now within his grasp. What Sandi could not forget has been forgiven. What Hannah could not find has been revealed, and what we have never deserved has been offered. From the once-barren branches of our past comes nonperishable fruit. This is what grace does. This is who God is.

> *The hands that reached through time*
> *No beginning and no end*
> *Ruler of the yet to come*
> *And all that's ever been*
> *The One who knows my heart*
> *The One who loves me still*
> *The One who was and is*
> *The One who always will*
> *This is God.*[1]

—Clark

SEVENTEEN

Lord, Let Me See Again

Jesus said to him, "Receive your sight; your faith has saved you."
Immediately he regained his sight and followed him,
glorifying God; and all the people, when they saw it,
praised God (Luke 18:42-43).

Like most kids, I didn't necessarily enjoy going to the doctor when I was younger, even though, in my case, I seemed to spend a disproportionate amount of time there. I determined early on that an appointment time was merely a suggestion and seemed to have little to no bearing on when we actually got to see the doctor. I also surmised that they spent so much time studying doctor-type stuff they were left with no time to fine-tune skills such as legible penmanship.

For all the not-so-pleasant memories associated with doctor visits, one thing I always looked forward to was getting to read a magazine called *Highlights*. To this day, I have never known anyone who actually subscribed to the magazine except for doctors' offices. It was not the cartoons or the stories I enjoyed, but a monthly feature called hidden pictures. For those who have not spent a lot of time in waiting rooms, this was a full-page line art drawing that, as the name implied, had a list of about fifteen to twenty objects hidden in the picture for you to find.

On a good day I would get to the magazine before anyone else had found and circled everything on the list. There was always a certain sense of accomplishment that came with discovering the answers all on my own, revealing what was once hidden, and highlighting the way for those who would follow. At least, that's what I told myself. But unfortunately, it didn't always work out that way. Sometimes it didn't matter how long I looked at the picture—I still couldn't seem to find all the objects.

To some this might seem a strange memory to carry around all these years later, and I would agree. In fact, I probably would have forgotten both the drawings and the hold they had on me were it not for life's little reminders that seem to seek me out and haunt me still.

Optical illusion books are the worst. You know the kind I am talking about. Stare at the image long enough and you will supposedly see a school of dolphins or some other grandiose image. I really can't say with any real certainty, since the only way I knew dolphins were there to begin with was because the caption underneath the picture told me so. My frustration stemmed not only from the fact that I wanted to see dolphins, but also from the sense that everyone in the world could see the image but me.

Sometimes We Are Hindered by What We *Do Not* See

A few weeks ago I found myself in the uncomfortable position of sitting in a meeting that I was also the subject of. I listened intently as people I deeply respect began to lay out a road map for effectively managing the ministry God has called me to. The longer I sat there, the more obvious it became that everyone at the table could see something in me I could not begin to see in myself.

The spiritual analogy was there for the taking: God always sees something greater in us than we can see in ourselves. At times I have offered that truth as encouragement to others, yet there I sat, guilty of living beneath the same promise when it came to me. If everyone else at the table could see it, I wanted to as well. I could not understand why it seemed God was withholding the knowledge that would allow me to walk with greater confidence on a path I had already committed to follow.

I thought about Moses' reaction when God commissioned him to lead the children of Israel out of Egypt. Rather than being honored and overjoyed by such a call, Moses immediately began to protest that he was the wrong choice for the mission. He told God how he had never been very eloquent, and not only that, he was slow of speech and got easily tongue-tied. Surely God could not expect him, with all his weaknesses, to go before Pharaoh and ask for the Israelites' release.

I am not convinced, however, that Moses had a speech problem so much as a vision problem. He just couldn't see himself as one who possessed the gifts needed to carry out God's will. In Exodus 4:12, God even attempted to assuage Moses' claim that he didn't speak well enough by saying, "I will be with your mouth and teach you what you are to speak." After about the third or fourth excuse, God could have just turned and walked away, but he could see something that Moses could not see in himself.

For me, one of the key pieces of the story is how God eventually alleviated Moses' fears not by releasing him from the call, but by sending him a helper who was strong in the areas Moses felt weak. I love how God did not send a total stranger, but instead chose his brother Aaron, someone already in the inner circle.

The takeaway of the meeting that day was that even though God's voice was clear and his call was obvious, he also loved me enough to listen patiently while I aired my feelings of inadequacy, whether real or perceived. As I began to look around the table, I realized that God had surrounded me with not only one Aaron, but with another and another and another—brothers and sisters in Christ, united by God's call on our lives.

When the meeting finally ended, I felt an unexpected surge of empowerment—not in my abilities, but in an awareness of God's presence and purpose in the task at hand. Even though God was still calling me to do what I could not do on my own, he had already enlisted those who would come alongside of me. Together we would walk by faith into the mystery of God's promise.

Sometimes We Are Hindered by What We *Do* See

Maybe you too have found yourself struggling with a vision problem. But perhaps yours is different in that you find yourself hindered not by what you cannot see, but by what you can. Do you find at the core of your struggle the knowledge that buried beneath the fragile exterior, you still have an unobstructed view of an all-too-human past—sins long since forgiven by God, but not yet forgotten by you?

I am convinced that one of Satan's greatest weapons is using present-tense reminders of past-tense failures to prevent us from living tomorrow's promise. The lie of the enemy is rooted in half-truths. It tells us we are not worthy of any love, especially God's love. It longs to pull us down to the past as if grace had never happened. But here is the good news: grace did happen, and grace still happens. We cannot allow ourselves to be tricked into believing anything different.

Several years ago I was in Independence, Kansas, for a revival meeting. One evening after the service, we went to the home of a family in the church for food and fellowship. As we walked in the side door, I was struck by what I thought was an odd visual. On the porch was a full-sized St. Bernard dog. Around the dog's neck was a rope about three feet long, obviously not attached to anything. Because it was a small porch and the large dog showed no intention of moving, we took turns stepping over him to get into the house. Our host laughingly apologized for the obstruction but never mentioned the rope.

As our time together ended and we walked back outside, curiosity got the best of me and I asked the question that had occupied my mind the entire evening: "What is the point of the rope that is not tied to anything around your dog's neck?" The man smiled and said, "Well, he doesn't realize he is not tied up. As long as the rope is around his neck, it keeps him from running off." The story might be humorous, except that we see the same principle lived out day after day in this journey called faith. Too often we live as if we are tethered to something that should have no hold over us.

Sometimes We Are Hindered by What We Cannot Understand

I remember hearing about a friend of mine who lost one of his legs in an accident. His mother described a unique medical phenomenon that doctors refer to as phantom pain—the pain still felt like it was coming from a part of the body that was no longer there. The problem was that the sensations were originating in the spinal cord and the brain rather than the leg itself, so even though the leg was gone, the feelings of pain remained. I remember thinking that even though I had never lost a limb, I could relate to the struggle on a spiritual level. Faith and Scripture tell us that our sins have been removed from us "as far as the east is from the west" (Psalm 103:12, NIV), yet our human logic says that cannot be possible.

Maybe you are familiar with the old saying that a person should never be judged by the worst thing he or she has done.

*God longs to take
a life once broken and
transform it into
something beyond
what we can see.*

The sad reality is that in far too many cases, the toughest verdict is the one we level against ourselves. We allow the failures of our past to become a lifelong sentence. They are a phantom albatross around our neck that leaves us gasping for breath beneath a weight God has already removed. It is a rope around our neck tied to nothing.

Aren't you glad the stain of failure is not permanent in God's eyes? Just as the soil must be stirred and broken before a seed can be planted, God longs to take a life once broken and transform it into something beyond what we can see. I think this is what the late hymn writer Julia Johnston meant when she wrote these beautiful words:

> *Grace, grace, God's grace,*
> *Grace that will pardon and cleanse within;*
> *Grace, grace, God's grace,*
> *Grace that is greater than all our sin.*

It is this grace that paved the way for an adulterer and murderer named David to become a king. It provided a haven for a harlot named Rahab when Jericho fell. It transformed Saul, the persecutor of believers, into a messenger of the gospel. It took the pride of a man named Nebuchadnezzar and allowed him to be broken, restored, and blessed again to be used for God's glory.

It is this same grace that allows someone like me to rise above my weakness and take my place in the story. Like the blind man who sat along the Jericho roadside, my faith has saved me and my sight has been restored. I am no longer bound by what I can or cannot do, what I can or cannot see, or what I can or cannot understand.

How about you? Don't you think that it's time to let go of whatever is hindering you from God's business?

EIGHTEEN

The Power of My Weakness

Have you not known? Have you not heard? The Lord is the everlasting God, the Creator of the ends of the earth. He does not faint or grow weary; his understanding is unsearchable. He gives power to the faint, and strengthens the powerless. Even youths will faint and be weary, and the young will fall exhausted; but those who wait for the Lord shall renew their strength, they shall mount up with wings like eagles, they shall run and not be weary, they shall walk and not faint (Isaiah 40:28-31).

Now, I'm not ready to admit whether I do or do not believe theories about birth order characteristics. Scientific studies point to several personality traits that are connected to birth order. Most of the studies I have read, however, come with qualifications like the following: A second-born child is most likely to exhibit qualities a, b, and c unless that second-born happens to be the opposite sex of the firstborn, in which case qualities a, b, and c are void because the second-born is not really a second-born, but a second firstborn. Confused? So are the people who do these studies, apparently.

Using my own completely unscientific research on how birth order determines personalities, I have come to some very strong conclusions. There is something unique about second-born children. I base this conclusion primarily on careful observation of two individuals—myself and my daughter Anna.

Anna has been a series of surprises since the day we brought her home from the hospital. She came equipped with her own brand of stubbornness and was not afraid to use it. As her personality began to blossom, we knew we were all in for an interesting ride. She has not let us down.

One day when she was five years old, I was walking through the living room with a piece of white poster board. Anna inquired as to what I was carrying and then answered her own question. She said, "Oh, I see! It's a picture of a polar bear smiling really big." I decided then that I too wanted to see the polar bears where everyone else saw only a poster board.

She surprised us by writing and illustrating her first book when she was nine and subscribing to *Bride* magazine with her own money at twelve. She surprised us again when she adopted the word "festive" as her new middle name. She never met a pun she wouldn't use or an extra hour's sleep she wouldn't take advantage of. In other words, Anna may look like her mother, but she's got a whole lot of her daddy going on. She is a dreamer at heart, and I can only conclude that it must be second-child syndrome.

There is a different kind of "second" syndrome seeking to devour the church—a syndrome that deals not with being second-born, but with the feeling of being second-best. This struggle propels some forward even as it sets others back. Although we pray for God to bless the gifts he has given us, we sometimes find it difficult not to compare our gifts with someone else's.

In the music industry, success is often measured by the number of awards hanging on the wall or credits on a résumé. In the church, we tend to look at Sunday morning head counts and financial statements. While it is good and even healthy to have some measureable successes, I think God is much more interested in the things that are immeasurable—a soul added to the kingdom through a sermon you don't remember preaching; a witness to a stranger in the produce aisle; an email sent to one that was forwarded to another. Could it be that one of heaven's many surprises will be the number of saints who are there through the faithfulness of those who never preached on TV, wrote a best-selling book, or had a gold record on the wall?

Several years ago I attended a high school reunion that represented a decade's worth of students from our small rural community. I made some new friends, saw people I used to know well, and ran into some who claimed to be old friends but did not look familiar. There were those who had aged well and others who . . . well, let's say they appeared biologically challenged. The stories of the evening seemed to center around grandchildren, countdowns to retirement, and parents who had passed.

Some of the best parts of the evening were the conversations with those anxious to share their conversion experiences with me. I initially suspected it might have been the coat I was wearing, which made me look somewhat preacher-ish. As it turned out, they had remembered my faith from high school and wanted to share what God had done in their lives as well. To think—I almost didn't go to the reunion out of fear it would dredge up all those feelings of being second-best.

My friend Tonni, who emceed the evening, unknowingly said something that might have been meant specifically for me. She said, "It doesn't matter who you were in high school, the most popular, the shyest . . . it is who you are today that matters." If that was the case at a high school reunion, I am even more thankful the same holds true in my walk with the Lord.

So who am I today? I am one of God's called, yet one still prone to feeling second-best. Never has that been more apparent than in the days and nights spent chasing this manuscript. I am convinced, however, that the nature of my struggle is the very thing that qualifies me to offer this book.

Someone asked me awhile back how my autobiography would read if I had only fifty words or fewer to tell it. I close with my response:

I have been blessed with family.

I have been trusted with pain.

I have been generous with belief.

I have been vulnerable with my heart.

I have experienced the wonder of life.

I have been loved by the Creator.

I have learned to live in the power of my weakness.

Notes

Chapter 4

1. *Underdog Theme*
Words and Music by Watt Biggers, Chester Stover, Joseph Harris and Treadwell Covington
Copyright © 1964 CLASSIC MEDIA MUSIC, INC.
Copyright Renewed
All Rights in the United States and Canada Administered by UNIVERSAL—POLYGRAM INTERNATIONAL PUBLISHING, INC.
All Rights Reserved. Used by Permission
Reprinted by Permission of Hal Leonard Corporation

Chapter 11

1. Dave Clark, Donald Koch, Greg Long, "In the Waiting." Copyright © 2001 Word Music, Inc./Curlin Music. All rights reserved. Used by permission.

Chapter 15

1. Rhea Miller, "I'd Rather Have Jesus," words copyright © 1922, renewed 1950; music copyright © 1939, renewed 1966 by Chancel Music, Inc, assigned to The Rodeheaver Co. (a div. of Word, Inc.). All rights reserved. Used by permission.

Chapter 16

1. Dave Clark, "This Is God," copyright © 2013 Pilot Point Music (ASCAP). All rights reserved. Used by permission.

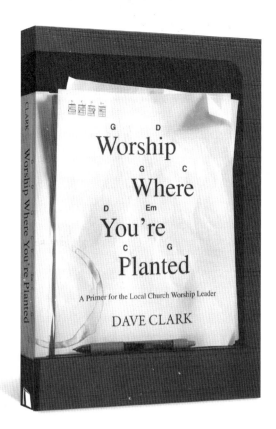

Worship Where You're Planted seeks to recognize and respond to the situations that worship leaders encounter. Through exploration and insight, author Dave Clark tackles issues such as transitioning between worship leaders, navigating between traditional and contemporary music styles, and building rapport with the congregation. With wisdom and understanding, Clark helps small and midsize churches find comfort and connection as they lead their congregations in worship.

Worship Where You're Planted
A Primer for the Local Church Worship Leader
Dave Clark
ISBN: 978-0-8341-2555-1

BEACON HILL PRESS
OF KANSAS CITY

www.beaconhillbooks.com
facebook.com/beaconhillpress
Available online or wherever books are sold.